THE STORY OF TOOLS

Pavilion
An imprint of HarperCollinsPublishers Ltd
1 London Bridge Street
London SE1 9GF

www.harpercollins.co.uk

HarperCollinsPublishers
1st Floor, Watermarque Building
Ringsend Road Dublin 4
Ireland

First published in Great Britain by Pavilion, an imprint of HarperCollinsPublishers Ltd 2022

ISBN 978-1-911595-70-0

This book is produced from independently certified FSC™ paper to ensure responsible forest management.

MIX
Paper from
responsible sources
FSC™ C007454

This book is produced from independently certified FSC ™ paper
to ensure responsible forest management.

For more information visit: www.harpercollins.co.uk/green

For more information visit:
www.harpercollins.co.uk/green

Printed and bound by Leo Paper Products, China

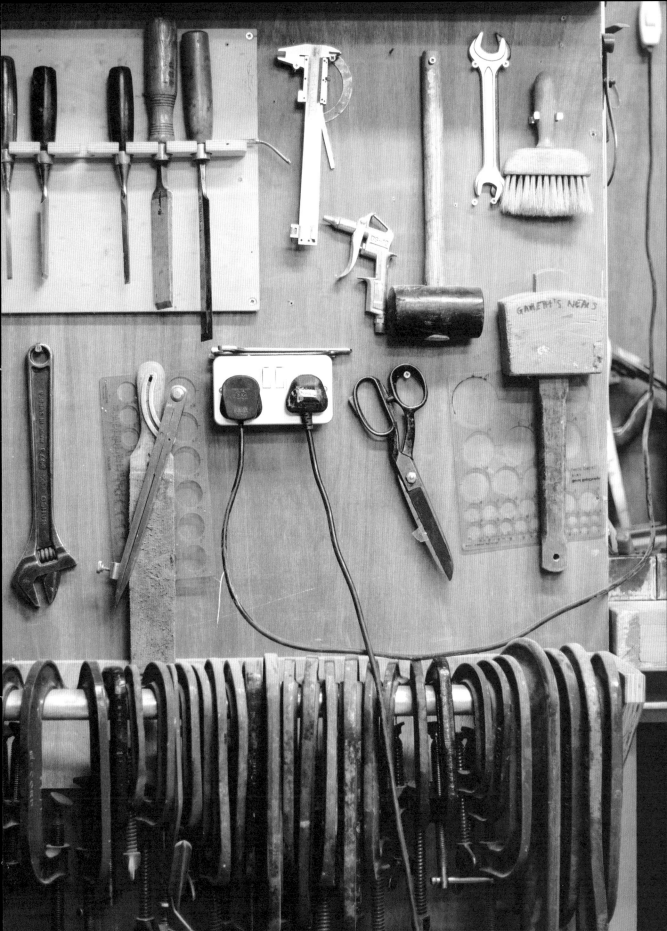

Contents

*'To do your job properly and
to get pleasure from it, you need
the good tool'*

John Stewart Collis, *The Worm Forgives the Plough*

The use of tools is one of the earliest defining moments in the history of humankind. In fact, it is arguably the very thing that makes us human. Our ability to fashion the objects around us – be they bone, stone, wood or flint – into the implements that first aided us in our attempts to hunt, eat, cook, make and build, mark a pivotal point in our evolution. Once prehistoric man learnt to shape the world around him to his own needs, it marked our difference from all other animals.

This book, then, seeks to explore our relationship with these most fundamental of objects – those that allow us to realise our potential as makers, problem solvers, doers. The best tools last a lifetime – or even several, passed down through generations from parent to child: a practical heirloom, cherished by its owner and often imbued with an almost mystical power, as if they are a repository for the knowledge gleaned from decade upon decade of making.

Those featured here vary enormously, both in terms of function and form: the well loved and well used; the simple and the complex; the adaptable and the single-purpose; the household and the highly specialised. Many are rightfully considered to be design icons, while others reveal the improvisational skills of their owners, tweaked and adjusted to suit specific jobs through trial and error.

Each chapter is devoted to a specific, unique tool, with their stories told by those who know them best – their owners, each recognised experts in their own fields, who wield these implements every day, or even make them to their own design and purpose. They have been chosen because each provides a unique insight into the making process, the ethos of the maker and our deeply held relationship with tools.

The word 'craftsman' is often used in slightly patronising tones: as a quaintly archaic throwback; an upholder of forgotten traditions in the face of the march of modernity. But, while this book is intended as a passionate ode to craftsmanship, it is by no means some Luddite attempt to preserve the skills of the past in aspic. Instead, these skills are firmly intertwined with the needs of today's creative industries – all of the tools featured here are being used, today, by modern craftsmen, designers and innovators.

Yanagi Sōetsu, the Japanese philosopher and founder of the *mingei* (folk craft) movement, proposed in his classic tome, *The Unknown Craftsman*, that an object is improved in the act of repeatedly making it. Take, for instance, the baseball bat: there is no single designer we can point to who conceived of it as an object. Instead, decades of improvements and refinements have transformed a simple plank of wood into the perfect object for its use. Likewise, many of the tools we use today – indeed even those that are utilised in making the baseball bat – are the result of countless tiny adjustments over time in order to make it fit for purpose.

At around the same time that Yanagi was proposing his vision for reviving folk craft, W. B. Honey, the British writer and authority on ceramics, wrote in his introduction to *British Craftsmanship* (1948), 'It is well known that people come to value a thing at its true worth only when they are on the point of losing it.' Honey saw 'the coming of the machine' as sounding the death-knell of traditional craft. Both might have been heartened to see how the craftsmen and women featured in this book are keeping those skills alive – not perhaps in the protectionist way they envisioned, but through innovation and ingenuity, while mostly using tools that they would recognise.

So you'll find craftspeople employed in familiar roles: woodturners, leatherworkers and ceramicists; furniture makers, blacksmiths and gardeners, but you'll also discover designer-makers, artists and even animators, who each have their own unique take on the tools they use day to day. These are the people you will find featured in *Hole & Corner*, a magazine dedicated to celebrating craft, beauty, passion and skill – to seeking out those spaces where creativity and inspiration can flow and helping it to flourish by talking to creative people who spend more time doing than talking.

In trying to establish what makes the perfect tool, this book aims to touch on a deeper truth. We live in an age of fast, throwaway culture, where we live our lives permanently online, desperate for the affirmation of clicks and 'likes'. All of which only makes us value those tangible moments of offline connection all the more. It may seem that it is becoming rarer and rarer to find these 'hole-and-corner' places (the expression comes from an old English phrase defined as 'a secret place or a life lived away from the mainstream'). But, as this book demonstrates, you can find them everywhere – you just need to know where to look. These highly talented makers are busying themselves in their sheds and studios, their kitchens and their offices, often working alone or in small teams – and, without knowing it, they are providing a model for us all.

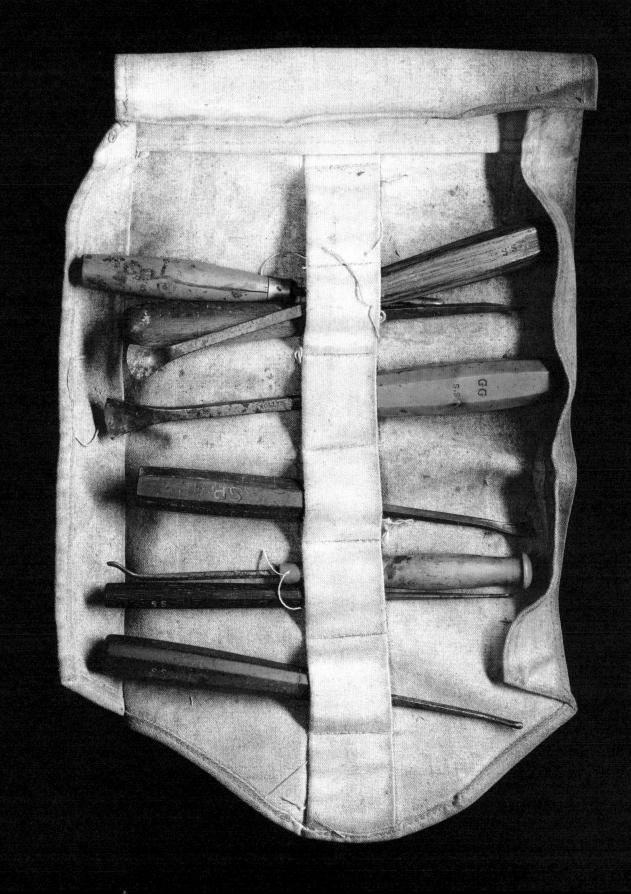

We are grateful to all the experts who have contributed to this book – for sharing their vast knowledge with us and providing an insight into their skills and techniques – but also for entrusting us with their tools, allowing us to borrow and photograph often priceless items that are their means of livelihood. This also includes the artist Linda Brothwell, who explains her own devotion to tools – and the unparalleled personal collection she has gathered over years of research from all around the world – over the page.

As blacksmith Alex Pole puts it, 'I find in working with these tools you can also transform yourself. You can advance yourself through your work, using the same process that transforms a piece of metal. For me, blacksmithing isn't a job, it's an integrated part of my whole existence. You're applying heat to your life and changing it – hopefully for the better. And in a sense that's what alchemy is.'

We hope you find a little bit of alchemy yourself in this book – the glimmer of inspiration that comes from a simple tool, used to its best potential.

Mark Hooper
Editor, Hole & Corner

Furniture maker and restorer Christopher Howe's set of carving gouges, collected over a lifetime from antiques markets (page 58)

Tools: An Appreciation

*Artist Linda Brothwell – originator of
Acts of Care and co-founder, with creative
studio Thirteen Ways, of The Tool
Appreciation Society for Hull City of
Culture – introduces her unique tool collection
and explains how tools enable finding
a sense of yourself – and of place – through
working with your hands…*

Tools are quite a wide subject for me. I make tools as part of my practice; in the *Acts of Care* series I make artworks in public spaces, but first I make the tools to create the artwork – so that involves design and inventing, and quite hard metalwork and woodwork. And of course I then use them. I get inspiration from discovering the tools that makers use in their practice – specifically looking at heritage crafts around the world. And through that, it unlocks the opportunity to talk to people about why they do what they do, or the heritage and history of their practice – whether that's them personally or in terms of their region.

It opens up the ability to talk to people in quite in-depth, personal ways. It can get quite emotional. But obviously you're looking down at a workbench, and people tend to be quite comfortable in that situation – you're using your hands to frame this conversation that can be quite sad, or personal, or poetic.

It's not just talking about the thing they're doing with their hands: it's the invitation of imagination. That's the thing with tools and why I make them; they've become a huge part of my practice. They're inviting this imagination of what's possible: what's possible to make; to repair; to interact with; to pass down, and as an exhibition object, it can be quite powerful.

We have a connection with tools still, I think. I have a huge respect for artisans and craftspeople. Although I work as an artist, I trained as a jeweller and a silversmith, so I come from that craft tradition and I've been doing it for more than 20 years. At the same time I'm quite future-focused in terms of things being able to adapt. The skills inherent in a particular process are so wide ranging that they can be streamlined and moved and adapted into another type of process.

So I'm interested in tools as a vehicle: as a way of talking to people about their lives. And from the other side, I have a huge collection of tools myself. But I'm quite wary of the fetishisation of tools; this kind of nostalgia on pub walls. It's a nostalgia that I don't think is helpful. I think respect is helpful – for skills and training and learning and dedication and caring for a place – I think that's incredibly important and something we should encourage and celebrate when we see it.

With my own collection, the tools I collect are either things that remind me of people or places, or unique tools that I don't understand. Amazingly I get to put my obsession with tool collecting under the banner of 'work'. I travel a lot for work doing research, so I'll tend to visit factories, makers, go on tours, go to fleamarkets, usually on my own or with a translator. If I find a tool I haven't seen before I'll try to find out about it, to get hold of it and speak to the person who uses it.

I'm a big fan of markings and measurements and weights. And I have a huge collection of hammers, partly because I actually use them myself, so I collect them to use rather than as decorative objects. They might sometimes go up on the wall, but it's just the wall above my workbench.

I'm creating space for the rallying cry of looking after things and working with your hands; finding a sense of yourself and a sense of place through doing that. And for me tools do that, and tools talk about that so well, because not only are they the objects they are, they also have this potential...

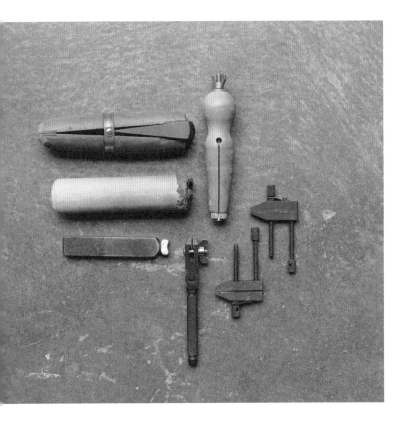

Part of Linda Brothwell's collection of jewellers' vices and clamps (above); and (right) various weights including stone, lead, a leather sandbag for silversmithing and brightly coloured board cleaners acquired from a school in Hong Kong

The Collector: Ron Geesin

*Pink Floyd composer, author and
self-professed 'neo-renaissance man',
Ron Geesin is many things.
But the achievement he's most
proud of is his unequalled collection
of adjustable tools…*

To fans of prog rock and psychedelic music, Ron Geesin is a minor but pivotal character in the story of Pink Floyd, as co-composer of their hugely ambitious 1970 album, *Atom Heart Mother*, as well as the producer of collectable experimental electronica, soundtracks and library music. But it's his own collection that brings us to his rural East Sussex home – because Ron is more interested in showing us his complex of corrugated sheds-cum-workshops, which house his huge, meticulously organised museum of steel and copper tools. Ron's collection is as gloriously specific as it is exhaustive. The title of his recent book tells you all you need to know: *The Adjustable Spanner: History, Origins and Development to 1970*.

'Why did I write it? Because I was trying to find a book about them, and there wasn't one – so I had to write it!' Ron has amassed some 3,000 spanners from the UK and over 1,000 from Continental Europe; a love fostered in his teenage years after he stole one from his father's toolbox, and became fascinated with the beauty of these strange, simple tools. He hasn't counted them recently. 'I'm never going to stop to count them now! And that shouldn't matter: once you get a certain way down the road, you can't stop, or you shouldn't stop. To do so you would have to sue yourself for bad representation!'

What matters to Ron is this: what the adjustable spanner represents in British culture – as a tool of our history, as a humble object of use, a crafted item for the ordinary worker – something that tells us much about the small details of our world. It also appeals to him as a man who is interested in the form and structure of things; of music and other forms. Or as he puts it: 'There is a pattern in collecting things and keeping them beautiful, isn't there?'

Born in rural Ayrshire in 1943, Ron Geesin has always had a fascination with making. 'I'd bolt meals, because I wanted to get back out to my dad's little bench at the back of his garage, to make something. Maybe I didn't make it very well, but it was the feeling of *doing* that got to me, there's no doubt about that.'

Geesin Senior had built the bungalow his family lived in, and the buggy baby Ron was pushed around in. 'By the time I was 15, 16, I was rebelling, doing surreal paintings, and generally annoying

'There is a pattern in collecting things and keeping them beautiful, isn't there?'

Geesin is fascinated with discovering more about the working conditions in which these tools were produced: '...it's about finding out about the lives of those people, and what they went through to do their passion'

'You actually need three to do most jobs, and once you've got three of anything – bang! You're a collector!'

my dad. He was priming me towards steelmaking, but something was telling me that that was all wrong. And I was, right, wasn't I? The steel industry's collapsed!'

Instead, music became Geesin's 'sort-of career' in the mid-1960s, when he lived in the heart of Swinging London recording experimental music and mixing with some of the stars of the scene – one of whom happened to be Pink Floyd's Roger Waters. In 1970, after collaborating with Waters on several projects, he was brought in to write orchestral arrangements for Pink Floyd's *Atom Heart Mother* – a role that expanded to a co-composition credit. With the success, he escaped to the countryside of East Sussex with his wife Frances – where they have lived ever since.

Once there, with time to tinker away at metalwork and woodwork in his sheds, Geesin's adjustable spanner collection began – by accident, really. 'The car boot phenomenon kicked off, and I was at most of them. I was looking for old jazz 78s, and instead I found these.' In his book, Geesin describes his spanners in his typically florid, funny, touching way: '[these] enticingly odd mechanisms poking their heads out of rusty buckets, their mouths imploring for air and light, and I was forever trapped in their jaws, gripped, wrenched in their direction, my life forever adjusted by their seemingly endless diversity of form.'

He particularly admired the craftsmanship behind these simple tools, and how they spoke to a certain period in Britain's industrial history – they start popping up in numbers in the mid-19th century, he explains. 'Making them was a small operation, and that appealed to me: either a fella in a small workshop who literally knocked out a few hundred, to big industrialists like Lucas and Abingdon King Dick, who would have one bench in one corner of an enormous factory to make them.' Spanners were adjustable because there was little conformity of nuts in those days: and so they provided a neat and adaptable toolkit.

This logic puts forward the adjustable spanner as an idealistic object, one that could work for anyone – although this is not so. 'You actually need three to do most jobs,' Geesin shrugs, wryly. 'And once you've got three of anything – bang! You're a collector!' Geesin's collection reached 'critical mass', as he puts it, in the late 1990s, when he found out about a collector in the Midlands who had just died ('I'm afraid to say I was onto the widow immediately'). Geesin still remembers his excitement at seeing unusual examples together, many of which he hasn't seen since. 'But that area, the Midlands, was the centre of industry, so that made sense. Here were all these spanners laid out on the back garden path, by the collector's son. Me tiptoeing through them, going, "Christ, I've never seen that!"' (He barely made the journey back down the M1: the heavier Northern spanners nearly did for his car's suspension.)

The more he collected, though, the more stories Geesin discovered – 'Vivid characters', as he puts it – from the inventor of the lawnmower, Edwin Beard Budding, to Joseph Asbury, who married his adopted daughter, to William Kilby, the coach-wrench maker who murdered his son. Geesin is fascinated not simply with adding to his collection but with discovering more about the working conditions in which these tools were produced. His great hope is to find a photograph of where these people worked, or some technical drawings under a bed, put away in an old suitcase. 'For me, it's about finding out about the lives of those people, and what they went through to do their passion, quite often disappearing without trace.'

Geesin is full of the obscure but intriguing facts that collectors revel in – how, for instance, despite Americans claiming the term 'monkey wrench' as their own, it was actually a name given to one particular style of English adjustable spanner around 1840. 'That style – and word – emigrated to America, with the human carriers, and then myths came out of America about how the name started.' These include the inventor being a New Yorker called Charles Moncky. The real reason? The style was the profile of a monkey's head. 'But because of the power of American influence in the world through the 20th century, something else happens.' His eyes glimmer. 'That's another interesting little study about how something starts and then it changes…'

Interesting studies about how things start and then change are Ron Geesin all over. But he's not planning to expand his collection any further into European or American models any time soon. 'Good God, I'm not that mad,' he beams. 'Well, not yet!'

Jude Rogers

Wood and Stone

The Axe

strike while the iron is hot

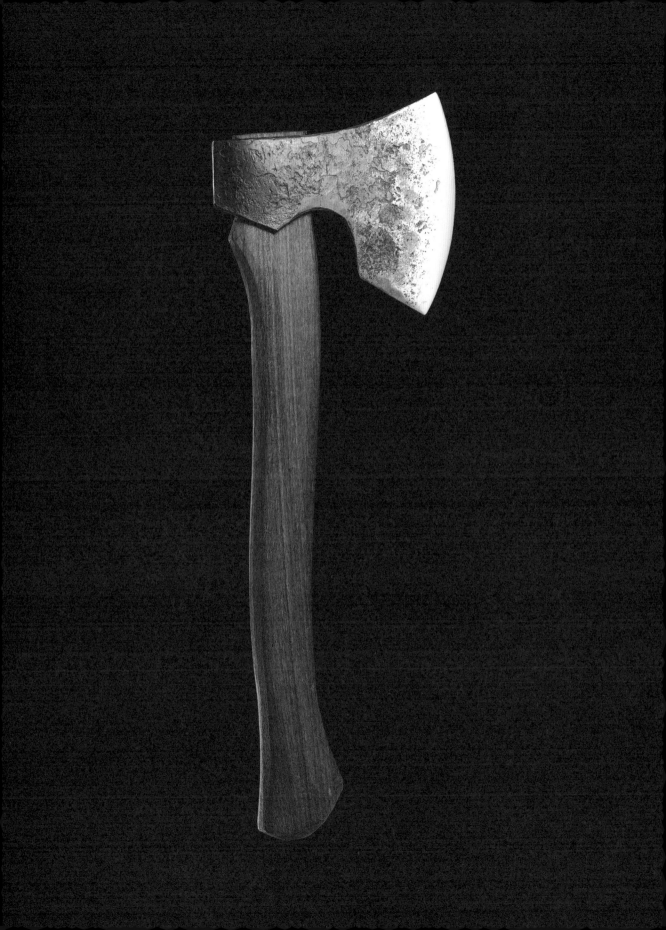

'We chopped down an apple tree the other day, the two of us with nice carving axes – we chopped it down into three or four pieces and stripped it in under half an hour. It's just a lovely feeling to be going out into an orchard with an axe you've forged yourself. I could have chainsawed the tree of course, but with a chainsaw you can't talk to anyone. You've got to put on your helmet and your gloves and your protective trousers, you're down there making a hell of a lot of noise – yes it's fast and it's efficient, but there's actually something remarkably nice about the two of us on a sunny afternoon, nattering away and working our way through it.'

Alex Pole is a blacksmith by trade, utilising a lifetime's training to forge kitchenware, hooks, keyrings and knives from wrought iron and steel. He has earned an enviable reputation for his work, and demonstrates his skill across the country at various high-profile events and festivals. But the aspect of his work that really captures his imagination is axe-making. Or rather, axes in general. There is a certain virtuous cycle in the process for him – he will chop down a tree and use some of the wood for the knife handles he makes, while the smaller pieces get chopped up and go into the wood burner he uses for forging. 'So you're making the tools, going out and using them – and then bringing back the produce as it were, the stuff you've chopped up, and then working your way through that to make more tools.'

His advice for anyone thinking of following in his footsteps? 'Don't get too immersed in the world of axes. It's a deep hole you can never crawl out of. The more axes I make, the more I want to make.' Still, you'd be hard-pushed to find a better authority on the tool – one who knows them inside out, from their raw material state to the finished product. So what makes a good specimen?

'Where it comes from is probably the main thing,' says Pole. 'There's a Swedish company called Gränsfors Bruks, which is where I trained: they make press-forged rather than hand-forged steel axes, but they're still regarded as some of the best in the world. So it's really about the provenance: whether it's machine-made or handmade, it's about whether the person who made it is taking care of the piece they're making; it's not just on a factory line. And of course what it's made from is also vital: if it's made from cheap steel, it will only perform like cheap steel: it will either get chipped or will go blunt very quickly. And then you need to look at how it's all fitted together: where the blade meets the handle. Lots of mass-production axes are just glued onto the handle, with any holes filled in with resin. For handmade axes you want to check the eye (the place where the handle goes into the axe) and check that there are no gaps. There should be a wedge in it that splays the wood out, so that it's nice and secure.'

And it's not until this final stage of the making process that you'll know for certain if you have a quality product. 'You don't know if it's a good axe until you put the handle on it,' says Pole. 'Obviously with experience you get a pretty good idea – the axe has to be hardened and tempered, polished; the edge is sharp, the handle's been shaped – but it's only the very last step, once you have the marriage of the two, that completes the process.' And even if the cutting blade is made to perfection and it's fixed securely onto the handle, a slight skewing of the axe head to one side or the other can ruin all the hard work, since you don't have a good lined-up cutting edge to strike with.

The use – and availability – of high-carbon steel, which becomes harder and stronger through heat treating, revolutionised axe-making. 'The traditional way of making axes is you'd have a lump of iron, which is soft and springy, and then you would cut into the face of it and insert a very small piece of high-carbon steel,' explains Pole. 'In medieval times, which would have been the heyday, it's said that high-carbon steel would have been more valuable than gold. Nowadays, with modern materials, I can take a two-by-four-inch block of high-carbon steel and forge a mono-steel blade: that would have been unimaginable at one time, simply because the cost would have been exorbitant. Some people estimate that a sword in the same material would have been worth the same as a castle. I don't know about that, but it was a serious investment.'

The particulars of axe-making reveal the derivation of the adage, 'always strike while the iron is hot', as Pole explains: 'Axe steel is quite interesting – the stuff we use comes from Sweden, where they still have a very highly rated steel-production industry. It doesn't want to be forged when it's too cold – equally you can't overheat a piece of steel, especially when it's for an axe: if you overheat the cutting edge then you burn the carbon out and it will become brittle and/or soft, depending on what you're doing to it. So when you're making an axe head, you're constantly looking out for a bit of colour in the steel and also listening to it, because the colder the steel gets, the higher the pitch it produces when you hit it. So if it starts to sound really high-pitched and tinny as you're hitting it… you probably don't want to be doing that too much. If you're just

softening the very sharp corners, that's OK, but if you're really striking it, you want to be building strength. And when you go to harden the axe, it can really split. You want the temperature to sit at around 950°C: certainly above 850°C and below 1,000°C.'

The cooling process is equally vital. 'I still have a master teacher who I work with and who teaches me,' says Pole. 'Twenty-seven years of making axes and there's still lots to learn. You need to normalise it. So you put loads of stress into it and, just like when you mix dough, with most high-carbonate steels, once you've finished making the piece you take it up to 800 degrees and then you let it cool really slowly, so you take all the stress out of it, and then it goes into hardening. And that's one of the most complicated things. When we run our axe-making courses, which are held over two days, a lot of the students think they'll be on the forge for two days, but you do one day of that and the rest is heat-treating and tempering and grinding – because otherwise all you've got is a piece of steel that just looks like an axe. The real life and soul is given to it when you go through this hardening process. That's a real art in itself. My master can judge the temperature of a piece of steel within about 25 degrees just by looking at it. That's hugely impressive when you're talking about probably a 1,000°C temperature range.'

As for care of the axe, it comes down to one simple rule: keep it sharp. 'Rather than waiting until it's really blunt, you want to test your axe every time after you use it: if you've been chopping wood for two or three hours you might have dulled the edge.' Basic axe-sharpening stones will maintain the edge, and then it's simply a case of wiping the head to remove any resin from the wood, as well as moss and moisture, and adding a bit of WD40 or linseed oil, ideally on the inside of the axe sheath – which is there not so much for safety reasons as for protecting the cutting edge from getting damaged.

Standing at 6ft 6in [1.98m], in many ways Pole embodies the common expectations one has of a blacksmith. But his attitude to all aspects of his work is very much about brain over brawn – as revealed by his preference for using a relatively light axe: around 1–2lb [0.5–1kg] in weight. 'When I hold an axe I want it to feel balanced and quite nose-heavy or top-heavy,' he says. 'A lot of people prefer a heavier axe because it chops into the wood quicker. But you don't want something that's so heavy you're wearing your arm out from chopping away for hours on end. Let the tool do the work, not your muscles.'

'Twenty-seven years of making axes and there's still lots to learn. I still have a master teacher I work with'

The Chisel
time-worn Swedish tradition

'A lot of what one does with a tool is about familiarity,' says Sean Sutcliffe, co-founder (with Sir Terence Conran) of the sustainable furniture and interiors brand Benchmark. 'There's the classic line of, "You're not a craftsman until you've done 10,000 hours' work" – but another definition is, "You're not a craftsman until you think with the point of your tool". Most of us will think as far as our hand, but then you put a tool in it, and that's a different matter! With extreme familiarity, the tool becomes part of your hand – your thought process extends through your hands to your tool. I'm doing it now, I've got my chisel in my hand and because I've been doing it for 40 years it just fits seamlessly; I no longer think about how it fits in my hands. In that sense, a tool that's been with you for a very long time does become a better tool.'

The chisels in question – and photographed here – have been with Sutcliffe for almost an entire lifetime. 'They were bought new by my uncle, who was a very famous wartime Danish sea captain and a keen amateur woodworker. I spent quite a few of my childhood holidays holidaying with him in Denmark and he shared his interest in woodworking with me. Before he died, he asked his wife – my aunt – to leave me his chisels. I didn't know about this until after he died, but she told me that he'd wanted me to have them. So they have a personal family history that lends them a poignancy for me.'

Made by the renowned Swedish maker E.A. Berg, Sutcliffe's tools (pictured here) are known as Shark Pattern chisels due to the shark motif on them, and are widely used throughout Scandinavia. 'The early ones in particular – as these are – were extremely good steel, so they hold an edge better than any modern European chisel I know,' says Sutcliffe. 'What I really like about them is their robust functionality. They're not the most beautiful chisels – they're not designed for that.'

Despite being paring chisels (which are generally lighter, thinner and more malleable – and used for shaving off thinner amounts of wood), the E.A. Berg designs are built as sturdily as mortise chisels (which are used for 'chopping out' joints and designed to be hit with a mallet, having a steel ring to prevent the handle from splitting).

'The metal ferrule on the handle is to allow them to be struck with a hammer,' Sutcliffe explains. 'Usually you just don't hit paring chisels with a hammer, but these seem to recognise the fact that they're a very workmanlike tool – and occasionally you need to give them a good thump. There's this contrast

'You're not a craftsman until you think with the point of your tool. Most of us will think as far as our hand, but then you put a tool in it, and that's a different matter!'

38

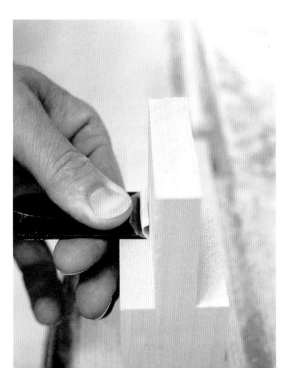

between a very finely made blade with a very pragmatic handle that I like.' Likewise, the handles are made of Masur birch – a local 'workaday' wood that originates from Karelia, a region that straddles parts of Finland and Russia. 'When people make really precious tools, they tend to use rosewood or boxwood,' says Sutcliffe. 'But I like E.A. Berg's approach – it's a humble wood, but in typical Swedish fashion, the steel is fantastic. And the bottom line is that it's the quality of steel that makes a great chisel.'

To connoisseurs of woodworking tools, there is another distinctive anomaly about this particular set of chisels: their peculiarly short, stubby profile. This is not, however, an original design feature. 'Of course, every time you sharpen a chisel you physically reduce its length – just by a fraction of a millimetre,' explains Sutcliffe. 'And so the stubbiness of the blades tells quite a story about their history. They're very, very well used. And every time I hold one, that sense of long history transmits itself to me. I've physically used them for 50 or 60 years – and they date originally from no later than 1950 – so they've been in use for nearly 70 years, and they've literally been ground down over time.'

Familiarity aside, Sutcliffe notes that these are not an example of a tool that intrinsically gets any better with age (they're certainly shorter) – but what has altered over time is the quality of workmanship that has gone into their making. 'In order to get a chisel of this quality now, you would either have to go to a very specialist maker, or you'd go for Japanese chisels,' he says. 'These are actually the closest things I've seen to a Japanese chisel, from a European toolmaker. And although I've also got a set of Japanese chisels – which I love – these are also the tools I used when I started professionally woodworking, from the age of 19, right through my training. They have journeyed with me: these have been my go-to chisels throughout my time as a professional woodworker. So they've got a long history with me personally; and they've also got a long history of association. I probably even used these as a child in my uncle's studio, without remembering doing so.'

The shortened blades can cause the odd frustration – especially in instances where they will no longer reach far enough when used in a particularly deep paring operation, but Sutcliffe notes that this is a rare necessity, since they are usually used for paring the shoulders of joints where you only need the front inch of the chisel. And in fact it has an added benefit: 'You actually have more control, because there is less lever: the shorter the tool, the less deflection or wobble there is,' he says. 'So if you wobble by 1mm at the handle end, with a shorter chisel there will be less wobble at the point end – and it's also less cumbersome to use.'

One last detail that Sutcliffe remarks on relates to the name: Swedish Shark Pattern chisels are so called because each has a shark symbol engraved on the blade. Except his set doesn't – instead, each bears a catfish engraving. 'They've always been called the Shark Pattern, but actually the early ones – anything that's pre-1958 – had a catfish. From 1959 onwards it became a shark. And actually the engraving of the catfish is a lot more detailed. Mine are catfish, not sharks: that's one of those semantic, nerdy points about them that I love.'

'They seem to recognise the fact that they're a very workmanlike tool… There's this contrast between a very finely made blade with a very pragmatic handle that I like'

The Drawknife
beyond the boundary

A traditional woodworking tool used to debark trees or for removing large slices of wood for flat-faceted work, the drawknife's thin blade is particularly useful in creating rounded surfaces and complex curves, both convex and concave. As such, it is a vital part of the cricket batmaker's armoury.

'The drawknife is my "go to" tool when approaching a new piece of willow,' says Christopher King, designer and master batmaker at Gray-Nicolls. The example shown here is a Brades drawknife, a British-made tool dating from the late 1930s, from King's personal batmaking kit. The main tool of a podshaver (the traditional name for batmaker), the drawknife is mostly used in this field to remove large amounts of wood in the preliminary shaping of the 'cleft'.

'With old bat shapes, it would have been used for pretty much the whole process, but the more complex profiles of modern bats require the use of finer tools like the round plane,' explains King. And he should know – Gray-Nicolls is famous for the 'scoop' – a hollowing on the reverse of the bat that reduces its weight without affecting its hitting power. King's own designs for Gray-Nicolls include the revolutionary 2013 Nemesis bat, created specifically for the more belligerent batting style of the shorter T20 cricket matches, with a silhouette that juts out at an extravagant, cartoonish angle both in profile and face-on elevations. ('I designed it with two basic criteria in mind,' he says. 'The first was that it should be recognisable. The shape alone should make it obvious as to what it was. The second was that it should look aggressive: it would look how the player wanted to play.')

While the drawknife has always traditionally been used to shape the blade of the bat – from the earliest curved examples from the late 16th century right up to King's Nemesis design, its versatility means it can be used in all aspects of the batmaking process. 'I also use it to shape the shoulders and ears of the bat – and it can even be used to shape the handle,' says King. (In fact, he uses a different, lower-quality drawknife for this job, 'since bat handles are made of cane, which blunts blades quicker'.)

Having trained in woodwork and started his employment as a furniture maker, King took to the drawknife immediately. 'It's a thinking tool,' he explains. 'It helps you get a feel for the material, or work out how it's going to shape. Each piece of willow has its own character, and you get an idea of how the wood is going to behave with the first few strokes of the drawknife. The response you get through the drawknife informs what you do next: the wood

'The drawknife is my "go to" tool when approaching a new piece of willow... It's a thinking tool: it helps you get a feel for the material'

may require the more guided stability that you can get with a plane, especially if the grain is being unhelpful. The knife can be quite a brutish tool in some hands, able to pull off great lumps of wood, but really it's a highly responsive, precision tool because of its simplicity – it's just a big blade with two handles.'

In practical terms, the drawknife is used – as the name suggests – by drawing the blade across the wood in a pulling motion, towards the body. By working along the length of the grain, the batmaker shaves the wood, using a skewed or 'slithering' technique, raising or lowering the handles to alter the angle at which the blade cuts into the wood.

'There's nowhere to hide with a drawknife,' says King. 'It's just you and the blade. There's no assistance from a metal foot, as you get with a plane or spokeshave. The reason a drawknife is such a good, responsive tool is precisely the reason some people find it hard to get the hang of: its simplicity of form offers no favours if you lack technique.'

Although the shaving action can take years to perfect, King finds it an intuitive and simple process. 'I had a lot of woodworking experience before I even picked up a drawknife, and I found it relatively easy,' he says. 'I think it's more down to understanding the material you're working with. If you understand the grain and know how the wood is probably going to behave, it's fairly simple to control a knife, but if you're new to the material, the drawknife will bite – or stick in the grain – and give you all sorts of discomfort. It's like most tools: if you learn the material, it's easier to learn the tool.'

King has certainly done his research: in 2012, the producers of the ITV drama series *Downton Abbey* commissioned him to produce historically accurate 1927-era cricket bats – which, compared with those used in the modern game, resembled straight planks of wood. But, however radical designs such as the Nemesis may appear, they still have to conform to the strictly defined Laws of Cricket, just as those in 1927 did: no bat can be more than four and a quarter inches wide, and must consist of a single piece of willow. (It's for this reason that Dennis Lillee's infamous aluminium 'ComBat' lasted just a few balls in the 1979 Ashes Test at the WACA in Perth before it was deemed illegal.) There are restrictions governing everything from the percentage of man-made material in the handle to the bat's overall length: in short, anything deemed to provide the batsman with an unfair advantage is liable to be banned.

Despite his role in introducing innovative new designs, King insists that 'the

'Each piece of willow has its own character, and you get an idea of how the wood is going to behave with the first few strokes of the drawknife'

game shapes the bats, not the other way around'. And when it comes to his tools of choice, he remains a traditionalist at heart. 'I always look for tools that are pre-World War II,' he says. 'The common belief is that, after the war, British steel quality dropped as our government tried to maximise profits on production and exports. You can tell pre-war steel, because it lasts a lot longer and holds an edge better. My Brades is beautifully balanced and feels good in the hands: the handles are ash and a nice simple shape. I've seen some drawknives with round handles like doorknobs and I can't understand how anyone uses them.'

Asked if there is anything he does to adapt or improvise the drawknife to make it work better for him, King is unequivocal: 'No. It's a matter of finding the right knife to start with. There's not much you could add to a good drawknife to make it better.'

'It's a highly responsive, precision tool because of its simplicity. It's just a big blade with handles… There's nowhere to hide with a drawknife'

Collections 01:

Carpentry

A selection of traditional planing, chiselling and
measuring tools for woodwork, as used by wooden
garden furniture designers Gaze Burvill.

Clockwise from top: pin hammer; tenon saw; sliding bevel; dividers; square;
marking knife; shoulder plane; Yankee spiral ratchet screwdriver; chisel

The Plane
sharp and flat

'There's this wonderful incongruity that old things are made better than newer things,' remarks David Linley. 'The old ones get better with age – they just do. Whereas the new ones just remain exactly the same. But I think, just as you play an instrument or drive a car, you become more familiar with the instrument or the machine. Therefore the pleasure increases along with the precision with which you play something or use it.'

Linley – full name David Albert Charles Armstrong-Jones, 2nd Earl of Snowdon – is the son of Princess Margaret and Anthony Armstrong-Jones (aka the photographer Lord Snowdon). He is also a grandson of King George VI and currently 20th in line of succession to the British throne. As a member of the British royal family, he is notable in having created his own viable independent business – David Linley Furniture Limited (now known simply as Linley) – specialising in marquetry, cabinetmaking, bespoke furniture, upholstery and interior design. Having developed his interest in woodmaking while at the famous Bedales School – renowned for its liberal ethos and progressive attitudes towards promoting art and craft – Linley went on to study at Parnham College, set up by the influential British furniture maker John Makepeace.

'At Parnham, Makepeace encouraged us beyond our comfort zones into the realms of excellence; those principles are still with me,' says Linley. 'I was taught by a wonderful man called Robert Ingham, who was the day-to-day tutor – as well as Greg Powlesland, who taught me more about old tools. Robert was very thorough. He made us plane our planes flat with a bit of sandpaper on a piece of plate glass for four days.'

The point of this monotonous approach to learning was of course to drum home the importance above all else of maintaining one's tools – and in particular to emphasise how vital the plane was to any woodworker. One of the most basic but also essential tools of the trade, it is used in shaping and flattening wood to produce a smooth, consistent surface. Although rotary power planers are today commonly used for larger-scale jobs (such as shaping or flattening large surfaces or boards), the more skilled work of fine-scale planing still requires the use of a hand plane. And the blade needs to be sharpened.

'It's about the finessing of what is already a very finely tuned tool,' Linley explains. 'But lots of people can't be bothered to do it: they've got the tool but they can't be bothered to fine-tune it.' The plane works on the basic principle of maintaining two angles – the 'primary' and the 'vector' – so that the blade cuts into the wood at the correct angle, while reducing 'chatter' (the jittery resistance that can cause the blade to catch) by keeping it as close as possible to the metal guiding plate.

'That was the one piece of advice above all else that sticks with me,' says Linley: 'the old adage of "The sharper the tool…" – so you'd use very specific sharpening stones – Black Arkansas, which is a highly polished stone, and a White Arkansas, which is more gritty. It's all about finessing what you've already got.'

The plane is all about consistency: shaving the wood consistently, at a consistent angle, in order to produce a consistent surface. It perhaps doesn't offer the same degree of flamboyance or freedom of expression that other woodworking tools might, but it provides the all-important groundwork that even the most artistic of craftsmen needs. (This is of course a gross generalisation, since it takes a great degree of skill to use a plane effectively, and a woodworker would usually have an array of different planes used in a specific order to flatten, 'true' and smooth a surface. This would typically consist of: a scrub plane, a jack plane, a jointer plane, a smoothing plane and perhaps a polishing plane. The polishing plane is commonly found in Japanese woodwork, and allows for even finer shavings. (It is also worth noting the fundamental difference between Japanese and Western planes: Japanese planes are used by pulling towards the body, whereas most Western planes are used by pushing away from the body, across a piece of wood.)

The example photographed on these pages is a chamfering plane – unique because it is designed to sit on the edge where two faces of wood join and cut at a 45-degree angle (producing what is known as a 'chamfered edge'.) Made from beechwood by Maples and dating from the 1930s, it belongs to the South London furniture restorers Gordon Maxwell.

The difference between an old plane and the design of new planes is largely one of ergonomics. 'The old planes have enough room for you to tuck three fingers around it and your top finger runs along the edge of the plane,' Linley explains, 'whereas the modern shape is much more based on holding it with four fingers – which would indicate the fact that you didn't know you're supposed to point your top finger.' In other words, somewhere in the mass production process, a design flaw has been introduced, presumably by someone

who doesn't actually use the tool. 'It's a sign of mass production, yes – and of dumbing down.' But while this might be symptomatic of an attitude that doesn't appreciate highly skilled, craft-based jobs, treating them as something menial rather than vital – and the general lack of attention to detail that ensues – Linley refuses to be disheartened.

'It's coming back,' he enthuses. 'We need to be optimistic and positive! At Linley we are all committed to the notion that, in this age of mass production and standardisation by machine, it has become more and more important to cultivate and preserve the traditional skills of the cabinetmaker and the marquetry cutter. Everything we produce at Linley is imbued with a certain Britishness: an inventiveness and meticulous attention to detail; an ingenuity and a creative spirit; a particular eccentricity, sophistication, wit and charm.'

And that begins with caring deeply about producing a perfectly flat surface.

'It's about the finessing of what is already a very finely tuned tool... The sharper the tool...'

The Carving Gouge
into the groove

Sets of tools may each have their own charm: the specificity of purpose that each individual piece represents; the dazzling array of workmanship and skill that they display as a whole; the symbol of professionalism and vocation that is laid out before us…

But often it's the stories they embody – the tale of how each came to end up in the same box, strap or pouch – that can prove the most fascinating.

'I think people have this idea that you go out and buy, say, a set of carving chisels in the same way you buy a set of drills,' says Christopher Howe, a world-renowned furniture maker, antiques dealer, upholsterer and interior designer. In fact, as his own personal set reveals, quite the opposite is true: a proper woodworker's tool set is acquired, added to – and indeed made – over a period of years, decades… even centuries.

'That's why they're so interesting and different and diverse – the shapes are all so different because they came from different carvers. In some cases,' he points out, 'the tool was made for the job.'

In other words, if a woodworker needed a tool for one specific job, say to get into a particular shape or a hollow in a piece of furniture they were working on, they would actually make the tool they needed themselves. 'You couldn't just go and buy it from the local hardware store; you'd have to make your own tools – and they'd often stamp them with their initials, just in the same way as they stamp the furniture they made with those tools.'

(Howe points out that one of the tools among his set photographed here is stamped with the initials 'GG' – and jokes that it may have belonged to the great Grinling Gibbons, the legendary Anglo-Dutch wood carver, renowned for his unparalleled work at Petworth House, Windsor Castle, Hampton Court Palace and St Paul's Cathedral. Given that he died in 1721, this seems unlikely.)

For his part, Howe (whose own creations can also be found at Hampton Court Palace, as well as The National Gallery, Sir John Soane's Museum and Strawberry Hill House) has learnt the importance of finding the right tool, having earned his reputation by learning his craft inside out – literally. Having studied sculpture at Goldsmith's College, London, he fell into the trade somewhat by accident, helping to restore furniture for his girlfriend at the time, who was a gilder. 'It was a brilliant way to get into understanding antiques,' he says. 'If you work for an antiques dealer or in an auction room, you look at furniture from the front or the top. But if you're a restorer, you

'It's not that we don't want to use modern methods, it's just that we tend to revert to the old way simply because it usually turns out to be the best way'

61

'You couldn't just go and buy it from the local hardware store; you'd have to make your own tools – and they'd often stamp them with their own initials'

'Early tools were ergonomic – they were an extension of your limbs and your muscles'

62

look at it from underneath and behind. You take it apart and you learn all the idiosyncrasies of those makers in, say, the 18th century – how each piece is different, how each maker made it in a different way, how it's constructed… And then you start getting into where the timber came from: you learn about it from the inside first. It makes you not just a different sort of antiques dealer, it makes you a different sort of furniture maker, because you learn how they made it in the 18th century, which is very different to the way they teach you to make furniture now.'

Howe still utilises the forgotten tricks of the trade he first discovered by taking historical pieces apart, bit by bit, and rebuilding them. 'We use a lot of the 18th-century joinery techniques here,' he says. 'We don't completely ignore modern techniques. If they're valid or if they're better – if there's a benefit or a point to them – we'll still use the odd modern trick or method. But what's interesting is how often there isn't a better way than the old way. It's not that we don't want to use modern methods, it's just that we tend to revert to the old way simply because it usually turns out to be the best way.'

And that, in turn, leads to an appreciation of the tools used by the past masters of woodwork – interpreting how a piece was constructed by the tools built specifically to do the job at hand. Howe enthusiastically picks up each tool in his set in turn, demonstrating the ingenuity of their design – how they can get under and inside intricate designs, whether used for producing fine piping or heavy gauging, finishing balustrades or chair legs.

'Traditional tools have this strange affinity with the human body where modern tools don't,' says Howe. 'Early tools were ergonomic – they were an extension of your limbs and your muscles. It's a really interesting point, because you're not in tune with the texture and resistance of the timber in the same way when you're using modern tools. Furniture makers employed different techniques and used different timbers because they were appropriate, in terms of their strength or weight. So these designs often comprised so many different types of timber in one piece of furniture. Nowadays it's all made out of one type. Yes, it was partly frugality and partly availability, but there was also a point to it: it was also to do with understanding the perfect qualities of the materials.'

Asked to name someone who still upholds those traditions, Howe cites Mike Sinclair (now his own carver under the eponymous Howe brand), who originally taught Howe at the London College of Furniture – and was his first employer, on model-making work for advertising jobs. ('Mike used to work with Charles Settrington, who went on to become Lord March at Goodwood, and was a photographer back then – and Mike was amazing at making anything, in any material.') It wasn't merely the carving skills Sinclair taught him that have proved indispensible to Howe's future career, either. 'He also taught me how to sharpen various carpentry tools,' he says. 'And one of the most fascinating of those is how to sharpen a very, very fine gouge. On the inside, you can use a bootlace with stropping paste, which is a fine abrasive used for sharpening the cutting edge and polishing. But if it's a really fine veining tool, you have to use a piece of linen thread to sharpen the inner edge. You hold it in place with your thumb and drag the thread through in order to sharpen it. Mike showed me how to do that fantastically, and that's been vital – because if you don't have sharp tools, you can't really do a decent job.'

But for all the practical advice on their use, Howe's magnificent collection of woodworking tools, gathered over a lifetime from various antiques markets – particularly London's Brick Lane and Camden Passage – serve another purpose. 'Personally I didn't collect these tools with a specific task in mind. I have used a lot of them, but probably only a fraction of those I've collected. I just love them as objects.'

'If you don't have sharp tools, you can't really do a decent job'

The Cordless Power Drill
with great power comes great responsibility

Some of the tools featured in this book have been passed down through generations; honed and perfected through countless man-hours of work and experimentation. But each represents the best (often literally) cutting-edge solution to a specific task. There is nothing Luddite in the selection over these pages: they are simply the best tools for the job, as demonstrated by the expert makers who use them.

So it is with the cordless power drill: the efficient, elegant, user-friendly answer to a centuries-old problem in the making process – how to fix two surfaces securely together.

Gareth Neal is a world-renowned designer-maker who focuses on furniture. An expert in the specialised tools required in his trade – many of which have been featured elsewhere here – he nonetheless claims the cordless power drill is the first bit of kit in his bag; the one he relies on most in his day-to-day work – and the most versatile. 'Though its functionality is simple, my requirement of it is endless,' he says. 'It is always at arm's length, whether it's for precision tasks, smashing together a shipping crate, or making a jig. It always goes with you for site work and is often used repeatedly throughout the whole day.'

Indeed, so vital is it in his arsenal that Neal will often have two drills simultaneously set up for their individual tasks. The simplicity of its design and ease of use also means anyone – from layman to seasoned expert – can put the power drill to effective use. 'Anyone can use one with a squeeze of the trigger, and this is another reason why it's so wonderful. It is also just as important at home as an essential for many a DIY task. But experience will enable you to use it more effectively and accurately.'

The model photographed here is Neal's own trusty 18V Makita drill. And while other manufacturers' power tools are also available, Makita was a pioneer in developing cordless technology for the mass market. Founded in 1915 in Nagoya, Japan by Mosaburo Makita, the Makita Electric Works company originally specialised in motors, transformers and lighting equipment. In 1969 it introduced the world's first rechargeable power tool: the 6500D battery-powered drill, which came with its own detachable battery pack – a vital element in cordless technology. The firm is also a forerunner in battery innovations: launching the first nickel cadmium battery tool in 1978 (the 6010D rechargeable drill); the first nickel hydride battery tool in 1997 (the 6213D); and the first lithium-ion battery tool in 2005 (the TD130D).

'Anyone can use a power drill with the squeeze of the trigger, and this is another reason why it's so wonderful'

'The power drill has eradicated the slow,
wrist-punishing tasks those old tools
came with'

But does it belong in this book? As Neal insists, it's more than worthy of its place among the other instruments in these pages because it fulfills the basic criteria that make up the very definition of a tool. 'It is perfect as a tool because it is something that enables a process or a function,' he says. 'It saves time, provides great results: form follows function.'

As for versatility – the possibilities of the power drill are endless. 'The name may describe its main function,' says Neal, 'but of course it also works as a screwdriver and can perform countless other tasks.' Moreover, it can be used to augment other handheld tools, providing more power to one's elbow when mere human motor skills aren't enough. 'Other tools can be held within its jaws, such as countersinks, cutters or allen-key heads,' adds Neal – a refreshing insight into the mind of a master craftsman, for whom the preciousness surrounding traditional making skills never outweighs the need to get the job done.

After all, every one of the aged, handheld tools featured in this book – often passed down from parent to child, carrying with them the muscle memory of countless generations of makers within them – were once the very height of technological innovation. Even the phrase 'cutting edge' recalls a tool at its most prosaic and efficient – while 'digital' likewise refers to the dexterity of the human behind the machine: it's not simply digits on the screen, but the digits that command them via the keyboard that is referred to. Why then shouldn't old ingenuity be coupled with the modern – or muscle power with the electric version?

'Its evolution from the humble screwdriver or the bit and brace into the modern world is also what defines it as something special,' continues Neal. 'Being rechargeable, it has eradicated the slow, wrist-punishing tasks those old tools came with.' It's not without its drawbacks, however – care must be used so as not to apply too much power to delicate tasks – many is the carpenter who curses the DIY enthusiast who has burred the head of a screw through the over-zealous use of a power tool, rendering it irremovable. (As someone said about something far more important: 'With great power comes great responsibility'.) For all his talk of wrist-friendliness, Neal does admit that there is the odd drawback to his tool of choice: 'I guess it is quite a heavy tool, and used without care and sensitivity you can make imprecise holes very quickly and easily,' he remarks. 'You do have to sometimes resort to the screwdriver!'

Collections 02:

Architecture

A set of pre-digital tools for drawing and measuring
architectural plans, once belonging to Geoffry Powell of
Chamberlin, Powell and Bon (whose work included
designing London's Barbican Estate).

Clockwise from top left: compass; set square; scale rule and ruler;
compass; drawing pen; charcoal set; magnifying glass;
French curve ruler; measuring dial

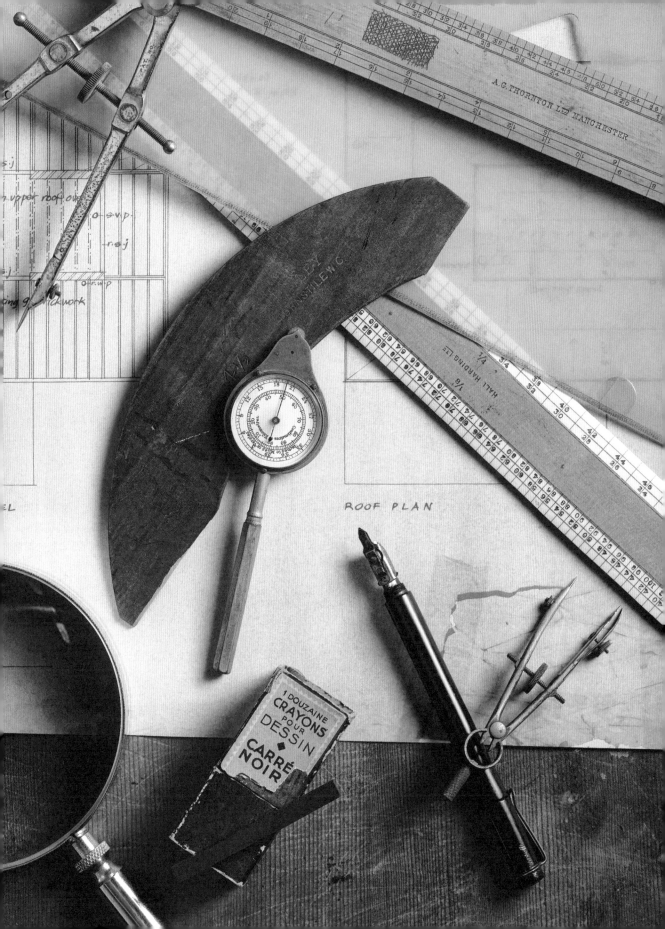

The Turning Hook
turn to face the change

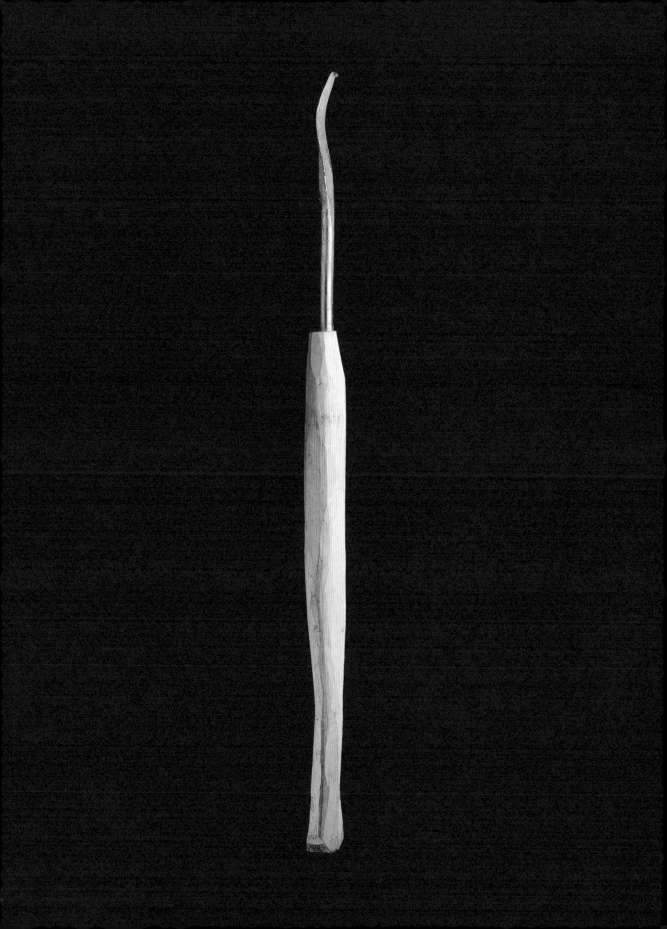

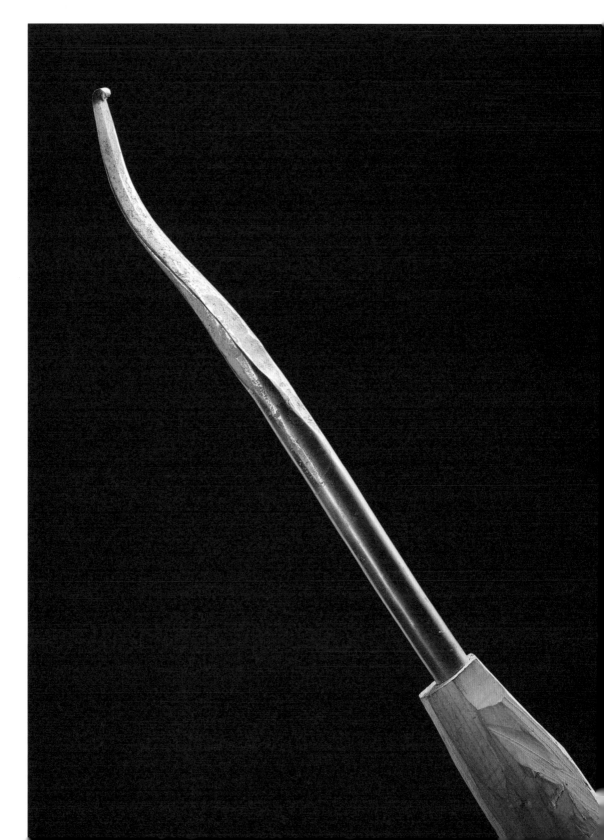

As the name would suggest, the turning hook is a hooked implement used in turning – specifically for woodturned objects such as bowls and plates. 'Actually it's a bit more complex than that,' says Robin Wood, who is a master woodturner and the founding chairman of the Heritage Crafts Association. (An advocacy body dedicated to promoting and protecting traditional 'heritage' crafts – defined as 'a practice which employs manual dexterity and skill and an understanding of traditional materials, design and techniques, and which has been practised for two or more successive generations' – its president is HRH The Prince of Wales.) 'I have about 100 of these hooks,' Wood continues; 'all slightly different, for slightly different shapes and sizes of bowls.'

And, as you might expect from a master of his craft, it goes a lot further – and deeper – than that simplistic explanation. 'The tool allows me to make nested bowls, which is the Holy Grail of traditional turning.' As Wood explains, it's not simply a matter of skill (although that is a huge part of the equation) – but also one of sustainability, that makes this such a treasured ability. 'By cutting one bowl inside another, I can get up to five bowls from one piece of wood – saving raw material, time and energy.'

For Wood (who is just as aptly named), the turning hook is a tool that is essential for his livelihood. 'Well I wouldn't die without it,' he emphasises, 'but I couldn't turn nested bowls without it. It's an essential tool for the job.' And, crucially, they aren't readily available via any recognised outlets – meaning that, before he can make the objects for which he is best known, Wood must first create the tools themselves – the one photographed here is one of his own designs. 'You can't buy them off the shelf, so realistically, if you want to be a traditional bowlturner, you have to learn how to forge these things yourself.'

As such, the idea of the perfect example of the tool is something that clearly keeps Wood awake at night. 'How long have you got?' he deadpans. 'It needs to be hard but tough, made from high-carbon steel – hardened then tempered.' The geometry of the cutting edge is also crucial. 'The hook should not be too big,' says Wood, struggling to put into words what he has an instinctive feel for. 'It's hard to say precisely what makes one hook sing while another just does the job OK.'

This emphasis on feel is something that is vital to Wood's vocation. 'When you're using this tool, the whole mental and physical output of the turner is focused on the cutting action of the tiny hook, which is buried deep out of

'You can't buy them off the shelf, so realistically, if you want to be a traditional bowlturner, you have to learn how to forge these things yourself'

sight inside the wooden bowl,' he explains. 'We progress by feel and experience alone – and never know the outcome until the last second when the core breaks out and we see the (hopefully) perfect finished bowl.'

This is clearly not a skill you can pick up in a day. 'It took me about five years to learn the basics, says Wood. 'Although I had no one to learn from.' Indeed the last person to use these tools was the woodturner George Lailey, who died in 1958 – when Wood was just three years old. 'Years later I saw his tools at the Museum of English Rural Life in Reading and started on the long road to learn the craft,' he says.

With no children and no apprentices to pass his skills on to, Lailey's profession was thought to have died with him: his equipment and tools were donated to the University of Reading as evidence of the last practitioner of traditional bowlturning using a pole lathe. Using techniques that had been passed down from generation to generation – he could trace a direct line of bowl-turning in his family at least as far back as the 18th century – Lailey never installed electricity in his studio, even when it became available.

Likewise, inspired by the expertise that was thought to have passed away with Lailey, Wood uses a foot-powered lathe, using elm logs that are first trimmed with a side axe to produce 'blanks' which are roughly turned into bowl shapes before being finished and hollowed on the lathe. This is done using the turning hook (sometimes referred to as a 'snake tool' due to the curl of the steel blade at the head) – gripping the long wooden handle with one hand while guiding the cutting edge by holding the metal at a pivot point ahead of the blade.

Despite his title as a master woodturner – and the support and patronage of HRH The Prince of Wales – Wood recognises that he still has a long way to go before he is the finished article. 'After 20 years I am still learning,' he insists. (Incidentally, pole-lathe woodturning isn't the only traditional craft that Wood has helped to revive: in May 2017 he was instrumental in the publication of the Heritage Craft Association's Radcliffe Red List of Endangered Crafts, identifying those skills that were in peril of being lost with the current generation of experts – through a lack of recruitment and training, exacerbated by an ageing workforce affected by the pressures of market forces on small, often rural businesses.)

But for anyone inspired as Wood was to adopt this unique craft, it is at least easier to get started today – something that Wood himself has taken pains to ensure, ironically utilising digital technology to keep such traditional handmade skills alive. 'I have put up YouTube videos showing exactly how the tools work and many folk worldwide are now learning how to turn bowls this way,' he says.

Not that he would ever be so presumptuous as to claim his to be the definably 'correct' way of using these ancient tools. 'I am always adapting and improvising, trying to make tools that work better, stay sharp longer and make better craft objects,' Wood says. 'Toolmaking is such a joyful, fulfilling, empowering thing to do. Even more so now that I make tools for others to use as well.'

The Spoon Knife
always stay ahead of the curve

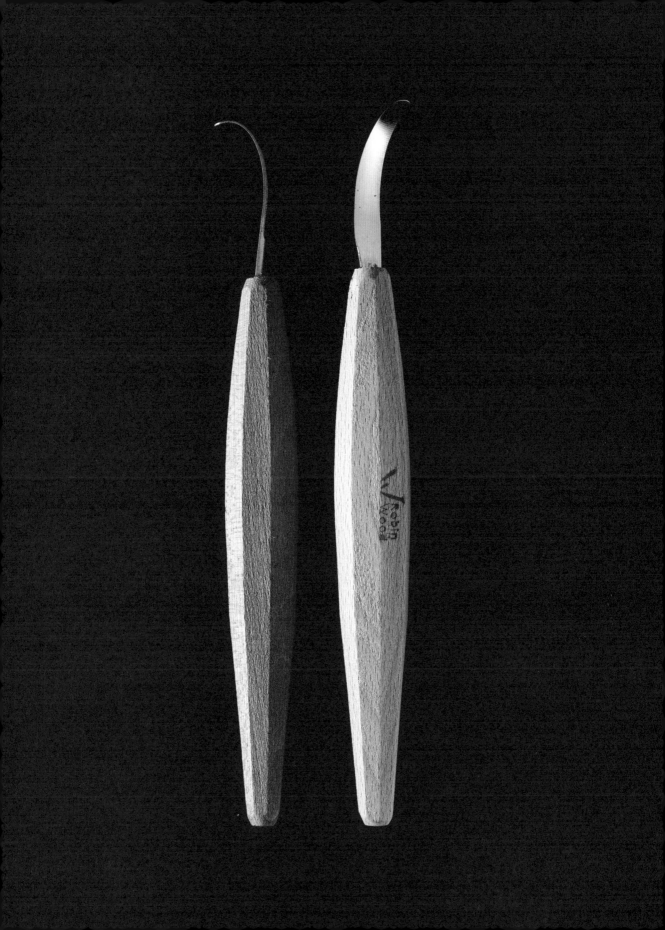

As specialist tools go, the spoon knife really cuts the mustard (or green poplar). It's the perfect example of the craftsperson's ingenuity in producing a tool that perfectly matches the specific demands of the job it's intended for.

'They did use stone tools for hollowing wooden spoons originally,' says spoon maker Barnaby Carder, 'but it would have been much harder work. A straight-edged stone tool compared with a straight-edged metal tool doesn't give you that much difference in terms of advantage: people think that metal's better because it's stronger, but the real advantage is that you can bend metal and form it the way you need.'

Carder is popularly known as 'Barn the Spoon' – which tells you all you need to know about his authority in discussing spoon carving and the tools required. There are many stages in the process of fashioning a spoon out of a single piece of wood. Robin Wood (see page 74), Carder's friend and fellow organiser of Spoonfest – aka 'the Woodstock of spoon making' – recommends using 'willow (*Salix*), poplar (*Populus*), alder (*Alnus*) and lime (*Tilia*) – basswood in the US. These are the softest of the hardwoods. These woods carve really easily when freshly cut or green and make excellent cooking and serving spoons.' This then needs to be roughly axed into a shape that approximates that of a spoon, before a variety of knives are used to whittle the wood, finessing it into a recognisable eating implement. But it is the spoon knife that, in Carder's words, provides 'the magic bit': the hollowing out of the 'bowl' of the spoon – that point at which a spatula shape becomes a recognisable spoon.

'That's the great thing about using metal, where you can bend the blade,' he explains. 'Back in the day, it must have been miraculous: people going from stone tools to metal tools that they could hammer into hooks and create bent blades.' (In his own idiosyncratic way, 'back in the day' for Carder identifies the point at which the Stone Age became the Iron age, with all the developments in manufacturing that rapidly entailed – in which the spoon knife with its radically curved blade becomes the physical embodiment of humankind's evolution.)

'The curve in the blade allows you to hollow out the wood,' says Carder. 'Obviously you can't hammer round a bend in the same way. It has this magical effect because, as you're working in a three-dimensional shape, you can sharpen a blade that would work on a flat surface, then bend it and it will work on a curved surface – which might sound really obvious but it's transformative.'

Although this is a development that was established between 1200–600BC, the spoon knife has seen some more recent evolution. 'When I first came into woodworking and spoon making, there weren't the tools available that there are now,' says Carder. 'I started using what is now generically called the *twca cam* – which is Welsh for "bent knife" – but what it tends to mean these days is a bent blade that follows a radius. Most spoon knives before I came along in the modern age were all question-mark shaped, so they had an accelerated curve. And I started using this one that is a complete radius. I did used to forge my own, but now you can get them from other makers.' (The one pictured here – that Carder uses in his own workshops and that he sells on his website – is made by the aforementioned Robin Wood.)

One of the interesting aspects that Carder picks up on about his work is how the tool not only shapes the object, but is in turn shaped by it. 'It tends to wear to the correct shape through use,' he explains. 'To a certain extent the outside of a spoon knife wears to the shape that it wants to be. So the object shapes the tool as much as the other way round. That for me is the fascinating thing about edged tools – they really are a dynamic thing; they're never the same. Because when you're using it and when you're sharpening it, you're actually removing a part of it – so it's always getting smaller. And those microscopic changes make a significant difference. And so you're learning each time you're sharpening.'

Carder declares that his love of the spoon knife is chiefly due to the unique cross-section of the blade and the challenge that offers to a maker. Taking the wood plane as a contrasting example, he notes how the plane has 'an engineered flat sole to it that guides the plane into the wood – whereas when you're using edged tools you're actually using the shape of the metal to guide the edge, so it's all in one, combined. And when you're sharpening it you're affecting that. Sharpening a plane, for instance, is much easier, because you can just get a sharpening guide, sharpen it to a particular bevel angle, and put it into the plane – and because someone clever has designed the plane, it's all set up: you just whack it in and it works. Whereas when you're using an edged tool, you have to do all of that yourself; you have to understand the angle of the edge and how it's built into the body of the spoon knife.'

Sharpening is, it seems, the bane of a spoon carver's life, due to the potential for spreading dirt and contaminating the end product. 'I like to do all my sharpening at once and then not worry about doing it for a week if possible,' says Carder. 'You can get really dirty hands from sharpening, and if that gets on

'The curve in the blade allows you to hollow out the wood… which might sound really obvious but it's transformative'

a spoon it's really difficult to get off. Dirty spoons are the biggest frustration, which is why I sharpen in batches.' Otherwise, for this most meditative of vocations, the only other frustration can be mould developing in logs as the green wood dries out – 'but it's just about managing that, and getting your timings right – a bit like a chef but on a slightly longer timescale,' says Carder. 'The wood won't last forever as a stack of logs – but once it's made into a spoon it does – so you just have to keep an eye on that and make sure you use the wood before it's too late. I suppose that's the Zen of the craftsperson, learning to go with the flow.'

Talking of a Zen-like approach, although Carder identifies the *twca cam* as the tool he uses most, he doesn't place any special significance on one individual example over any other, rejecting the favouritism or the superstitious approach found in many makers. 'I have multiples, I'm not sentimental about my tools,' Carder says. 'What I am sentimental about is the precious knowledge that comes with it – for instance the difference between what is razor sharp and what is a bit rubbish. And actually how it's sharpened is what's important more than anything else – more than the style or the manufacturer. That knowledge – how to sharpen it properly – is what's really precious. I don't hold the tools themselves as precious, although there may be particular ones I'll go to more often than others just because the handle fits that little bit better. At the end of the day, if any of my tools vanished, I wouldn't be fussed at all. And that's very empowering.'

Earth, Metal and Glass

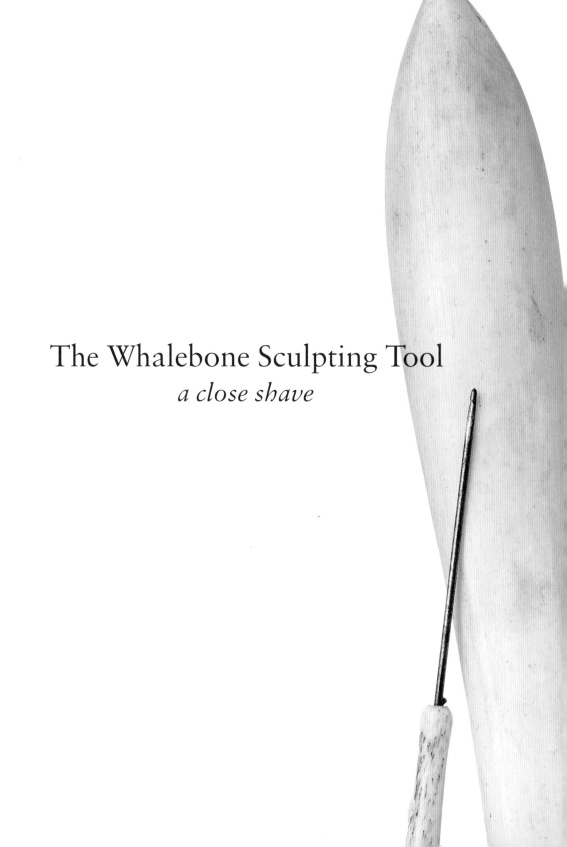

The Whalebone Sculpting Tool
a close shave

Improvisation can often be just as vital a part of the maker's toolkit as any individual instrument, and this can particularly be the case in areas of the creative arts that are relatively new.

Take, for instance, clay animation: although an established art, there is no firm rulebook concerning working practices, no centuries-old traditions to respect – let alone a definitive set of standardised tools that all makers use. While this may not be the case for traditional clay sculpture, the nature of animation offers its own particular and unique demands.

'People who've had classic training in fine arts have something of an advantage for a more natural sculpt, but for cartoon work, it needs to be in you to a degree,' says Jim Parkyn, senior model maker at Aardman Animations, the Oscar-winning firm behind the *Wallace & Gromit* franchise as well as the popular *Creature Comforts* and *Shaun the Sheep* series.

'Being able to breathe life into it is something that can't really be taught – you either have it or you don't. You can be a very good technical sculptor and have weird, lifeless mannequin-like creations, and then you can have slightly rougher, more characterful work, more life-filled characters – and that's where I come in. I'm famed for my funny animals really – the reason I did so well with things like *Creature Comforts* was turning out funny animals all day every day – that was my reason really for working.'

As you might expect, there are no agreed tools for breathing life into funny animals made of clay – and so Parkyn has developed his own typically esoteric collection, many adopted through trial and error. 'I have an interesting concoction of tools, some of which are made entirely from scratch,' he says. 'Others are based on old Victorian bone crochet hooks or even bits of corsetry made from whalebone – there's something very beautiful and smooth and polished about the material itself, something that lends itself to gliding through clay and making really clean marks, which is the thing that drew me to it.'

Although intended for an entirely different purpose, there are unique qualities to whalebone that makes it ideal for Parkyn's unusual line of work. 'I have a fine collection of newer tools – traditionally sculpting tools were made from highly polished metal, which is really nice to work with – and boxwood tools as well,' he says. 'But the quality seems to have dropped off over the past 10 years or so, and you find yourself frustrated, having to rework modern

There are no agreed tools for breathing life into funny animals made of clay
– and so Parkyn has developed his own typically esoteric collection, many
adopted through trial and error

Jim Parkyn's improvised approach means that, whatever the challenge, he has the tool for the job at hand

tools quite often to make them do what you want them to do. And you work quite peripatetically in this job, so you lose tools along the way and in trying to replace them you have to do so much work to them that it's almost worth starting from scratch anyway – heating them up and practically forging them yourself. And that's where the bone tools came in, because you can make them exactly how you want using sandpaper, knives and files – and make something relatively cleanly and quickly.'

This ability to improvise not just what is used as a tool but to also – in Parkyn's words – 'mould it into your hand' means that his toolbox is full of modified instruments: some altered to meet a specific requirement; some through running repairs. 'Some of my tools are held together by bits of brass tubing where I've done something stupid and put too much pressure on them, or couldn't be bothered to find a screwdriver to open a pot of paint and ended up snapping the tool in half,' he says. 'But that make-do-and-mend approach makes them look more interesting along the way as well.'

This creative approach to the tools of creation have resulted in a few distinctive designs that are all Parkyn's own. 'There's a shaving tool that I'm famed for in a way,' he says. 'It's a combination of a nice bone handle and a filed staple that's a mini razor essentially. I spend a lot of time cleaning the surfaces of clay or plasticine, trying to get the dirt off using this tiny razor. I became semi-famous during the 2010 World Cup, because *Shaun the Sheep* was one of the first HD animations in the world, and I was interviewed as part of the BBC's celebration of HD television – and the bit of footage they decided to use out of an hour's worth of interview was of me shaving a clay pig. Before every BBC football match – all the half-time and post-match analysis – there would be this two-minute clip of me talking about shaving pigs. I'd get people shouting "Pig shaver!" at me in the street. So I had my moment in the spotlight – although it wasn't quite what I was expecting!'

The introduction of HDTV technology has meant that there is no hiding place for the careless craftsman: every blemish and mistake is there for all to see. Previous tricks of the trade, such as using crude cardboard cut-outs as backdrops on set, are no longer an option. 'High definition will pick those things up in really upsetting detail,' says Parkyn. 'So you have to really up your game: everything has to be a lot more together. There's less "botch it" and more craft, so it's added a level of perfection on top of what was already quite an exact art.' The nature of clay animation work also means that model makers need to be versatile in terms of scale. 'It could be anything from a couple of inches high for the bunny in *The Curse of the Were-Rabbit*, to sculpting a whale over a fibreglass shell that's about six foot long by four foot high.'

Whatever the challenge – be it using whalebones to carve fake whales or shaving clay sheep – Parkyn's improvised approach means he has the tool for the job at hand. And, crucially, he never loses sight of the end result and the need to 'keep things funny and sunny' (to quote a phrase that has become something of a motto at Aardman).

'To a degree you keep the thumbprints in there,' says Parkyn. 'But sometimes you're looking for a much more natural or pristine feel, where you want that controllable finish. And that's what these tools give you, really.'

'There's something very beautiful and smooth and polished about the material itself, something that lends itself to gliding through clay and making really clean marks'

The Silver Hammer
earning a raise

'There's nothing more fulfilling than starting with a crisp sheet of machined metal and creating another natural form out of that. Machined objects are quite cold to me. I'm trying to order the material, but it has a natural chaos as well. It's not perfect – but I don't see the point in making a perfect object.'

Ndidi Ekubia is a contemporary silversmith based in London who has been making silverware under her own name for 20 years, using traditional hand-raising techniques (beating sheet metal over steel and wooden forms) and adding intricate detailing to the surface. As such, you could accurately describe her as something of an expert on hammers.

'I have certain hammers that I use all the time,' she says. 'Obviously everyone has their favourite tools, and I'm forever looking for the old ones – so they've all got a bit of a history. I've got one that I've used for so many years that I've had to change the handle several times, because it gets a good beating.'

Ekubia is largely self-taught, having studied three-dimensional design at the University of Wolverhampton, where she discovered a soundproof room with traditional hammers hung up on the walls. 'I just went in there and started playing with flat sheets, not realising what that trade was,' she recalls. 'And I've just refined my skills over the years.'

The making process itself involves raising up from a flat sheet – usually a disc of silver. 'The first stage is to 'block out' using the bowl end of the hammer to create the basic dish shape,' she says. 'Then you raise it using a raising hammer, which has a rectangular head. What you're doing is pushing the material into itself. You're hammering in a particular sequence. You get that rhythm – when I've been hammering for a while, I get lost in it – it's like a meditation. It's all about a consistent, rhythmical hammering – especially when I'm raising it up into its form. And then there's a different type of hammering for the patterns you create on the surface.'

Once she has produced the basic shape (she specialises in creating vessels including goblets, vases, bowls and ice buckets), Ekubia will use various hammers to achieve different effects in the design, eking out her distinctively intricate, rippled patterns in the silver. 'It's like handwriting,' she says; 'everyone will have a different style.'

During raising, Ekubia tends to hold the hammer near the end of the handle. 'My technique of hammering is quite fast, using the weight of the hammer to do most of the work,' she says. 'If you hold the hammer closer to the head, there's less swing, and if they're too heavy you'll get really tired very quickly.'

The balance point is usually controlled by the lengths of the hammer – a longer hammer allows you to get the balance exactly right as you swing it, whereas shorter hammers are used on work where not so much swing is needed.

The actual handles of her silversmithing hammers are of a standard length and shape – some will have a traditional bell-shaped end that means it fits in your hand easily and prevents it from slipping out of your grip while you are swinging it; others are relatively straight. But Ekubia doesn't expend too much energy thinking about or adapting the handles of her tools to make them fit better in her hand, preferring to concentrate on the business end. 'Everyone has their own shapes that suit them,' she says. 'For me, it's more about the actual hammerhead itself: the steel part of the hammer where you strike. That's what gets more attention and I'll keep it really highly polished.'

Or not. 'If you see a bit of masking tape on the end of one of my hammers, it's usually because I've not spent time to clean it up,' she admits. 'It just means I don't accidentally mark up the work from using a dirty hammer.' Scratches on the steel can easily mark the piece, and any bits of dust or dirt can get hammered into the metal, and so polishing the heads is vital to keep them clean and clear from scratches. 'I'm quite basic really: a lot of people use polishing machines, but I still use Wet and Dry Polishing Paper – and a bit of methylated spirits to clean it.'

Likewise, she will keep everything separate to avoid contamination. 'So if I'm grinding steel – or any other material besides silver – I'll keep it away from the silver pieces. Any particles that contaminate the surface can actually bore holes in the silver over a period of time, so you have to be careful.'

Time is the one frustration for her. 'Everything takes a long time,' she says. 'Especially because a lot of the things I make are one-offs. So it all takes forever. But I give the work the time that's needed because I'm a bit of a perfectionist when it comes down to design and making. And I've been lucky: people will pay for the work. They love it and they use it and they engage with it. It's been more than 20 years now, and I have had the opportunity to teach and see how other silversmiths have worked, and to compare practices.

Ekubia notes that, in terms of raising specifically, she is still in a minority as a female in the trade. Not that she finds that off-putting. 'I never get intimidated – remember I'm a girl who spends her time hammering metal all day!'

Collections 03:

Ceramics

A selection of tools used in throwing,
turning and shaping ceramics, as used
by potter Florian Gadsby.

Clockwise from top left: looped turning tool; wire; serrated kidney; a second
looped turning tool; metal throwing rib; turning tool; hole puncher; chamois
leather; wooden throwing rib

Glassmaking Jacks
a blow for opportunism

'There are a few basic glassmaking tools that haven't changed for centuries,' says Peter Layton, the founder of the London Glassblowing gallery and studio in London Bridge. 'Millennia really,' he corrects himself; 'they're all medieval tools or older.'

Now in his eighties, Layton is one of the world's leading artists working in glass. As well as founding London Glassblowing more than 40 years ago – the first hot-glass studios in Europe – he was also the co-founder of the influential Contemporary Glass Society in 1996. For all the tools in his workshop, amassed and perfected over thousands of years, it is the *pucellas* – or jacks – that he identifies as indispensable to his craft.

Essentially a sprung pair of tongs ('they're like old-fashioned curling tongs really'), jacks consist of two metal blades joined at a handle that can be squeezed to close them together. By controlling the distance between the two blades, the glassmaker can change the shape of the glass as it is rotated, separate the glass from the blowpipe, or flare the opening of a vessel.

'In the industry they used to have a different pair of tongs for virtually every purpose,' explains Layton. 'There would be one for opening up the glass from a sphere to a bowl; another for pulling out a stem; another for making a foot; another for making the neck of a bottle… a good maker could of course probably do all those things just with the one pair of tongs, but they come in various sizes and shapes so you will tend to find the one that best suits the job at hand.'

The particular pair photographed here comes from Layton's own personal working collection – and were made by the British blacksmith Ivan Smith, who specialised in creating tools for glassmaking. 'He is sadly no longer with us,' says Layton. 'He lived in the Black Country, in the glassmaking area around Stourbridge and Wolverhampton – and he was probably one of the most famous blacksmiths of his time in terms of glassmaking tools. He was there at the beginning of the studio glass movement in this country – which after all is only about 50 or so years old. His tools are very sought-after now: among glassmakers they are collectors' items. You'll find examples of his work in museums: they are beautifully balanced and aesthetically they're very pleasing to handle and use. The spring is in the handle, so it's a very simple squeezing action, but the quality of the spring is exceptional.'

Despite the simplicity of the design and the ubiquity of the tool, finding a pair with the correct balance is sacrosanct for glassmakers, and they will tend to guard a favoured set jealously. 'Having the right *pucellas* or jacks for a particular job is really satisfying,' says Layton. 'Obviously there are various qualities, but the really good ones have beautifully tempered edges, so they retain their profile and sharpness.' Despite this, jacks will tend to show signs of their age after years of use. 'I've seen pairs that have been used in factories for making thousands upon thousands of pieces of glass, and they will be all worn away, quite fabulous-looking in themselves somehow,' says Layton.

For his part, having originally worked in textiles after leaving school, Layton notes the similarity between glassmaking jacks and the cutting shears of the wool industry and the rag trade. ('I have a history with these kinds of tools I suppose.') But there is a magic in the transformative nature of glass that captivated him more than textiles ever could. 'It's the most incredible and seductive medium,' he says. 'It's malleable and alive, neither solid nor liquid. It's halfway between sculpture and painting... and you can also work with a huge range of colours.'

Indeed, Layton grew up with the artist David Hockney in Bradford, Yorkshire – they even went on a mountain-climbing holiday together when they were 17. The artistic side of glassmaking can often be overshadowed by a reputation for rather vulgar, ostentatious design ('glass is a Cinderella medium, overshadowed by ugly sisters,' admits Layton) – but he asserts that a new studio glass movement is emerging, 'opening up glass to a process of rediscovery and reinvention'.

The secrets of the craft have often been fiercely protected, with techniques passed down from parent to child. 'You'd visit Murano and they'd literally chase you away if they thought you were trying to steal their knowhow.' But Layton is generous in his willingness to impart his vast knowledge to the next generation of makers – which even extends to his readiness for allowing others to borrow his precious jacks. 'People do tend to have their own personal tools,' he says. 'I share mine, I must confess – and that's why I was slightly scared that someone might have taken a fancy to my Ivan Smiths when you asked to photograph them. I had to look hard in the studio for them. All glassmakers are pretty crazy about tools. They collect them, and you'll always find them rifling through these enormous toolboxes for the right tool for a specific task.'

By controlling the distance between the two blades, the glassmaker can change the shape of the glass as it is rotated, separate the glass from the blowpipe, or flare the opening of a vessel

Besides the quality of the making of individual tools, part of the reason for this protective nature is due to the fact that makers will adapt and personalise them according to their needs. 'People will certainly improvise a little with the blades – or at least keep them the way they like them,' says Layton. 'If for instance the spring isn't right in a pair of jacks, you'll tend to find a pair that is. Some people aren't as strong as others; some people like a firmer spring action; now and then, if you're doing very delicate work, I suppose you might want something that's quite soft. I remember a pair of *pucellas* by a company called Glass Equipment Limited in Halesowen near Stourbridge – they made them with stainless steel handles, and they had a double spring to strengthen them up – certainly people would have personalised those.'

Those aren't the only variables you need to keep abreast of in the job. 'You have to import colour bars or granules,' says Layton, 'and some colours contain precious metals. Reds and yellows often involve selenium, most of which comes from China. I remember one year the price of that went up 700 per cent.'

But, Layton insists, the appeal of glassmaking is that it is relatively fast – an equivalent ceramics job can often take months, whereas in glass a job can be completed within the space of a few days. And that is largely down to the tools: the ability to shape, mould and cut a piece of molten glass within the small window of opportunity when it is in a pliable state means there is little margin for error.

The Tickling Fork
germinating ideas

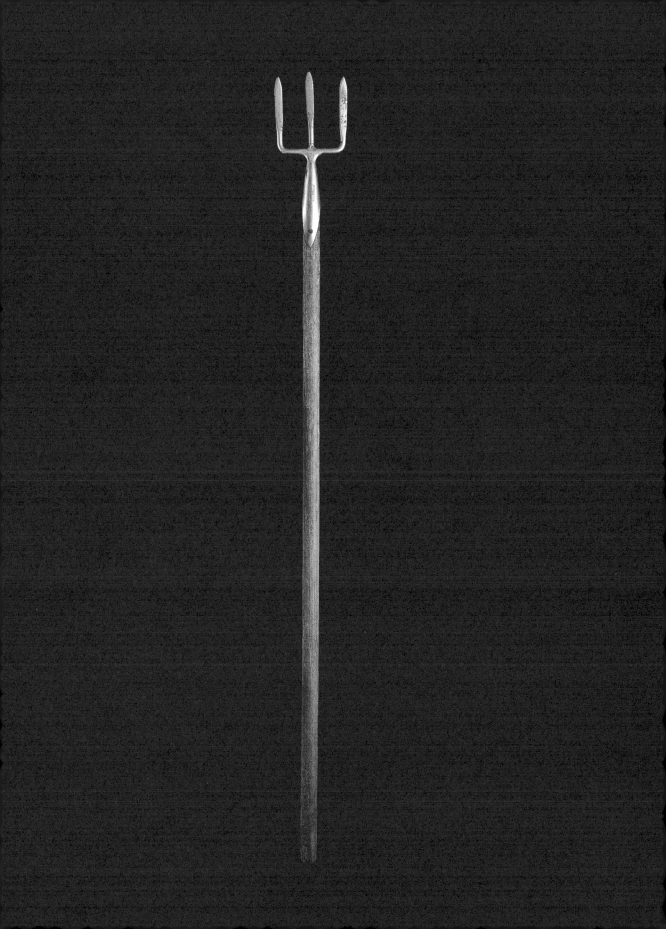

Sometimes the right tool for the job simply doesn't exist, and so you have to invent your own. As far as Fergus Garrett knows, the tickling fork is his own invention – even if the tool itself had already existed, designed for an entirely different purpose. Garrett (head gardener and latterly chief executive at Great Dixter House and Gardens in East Sussex) chanced upon a peculiarly long-handled but thin-pronged fork while on holiday, and decided to have his own set made to use back in Sussex. And thus the tickling fork was born.

The design proved so popular that he had extra tools made up for his team, and when members of the public started enquiring about them, they had more made by the Dutch family firm, Sneeboer, that are now for sale in the Great Dixter Shop. But as with all good tools, its inspiration came from a need for a very specific task.

'As a gardener you've got standard tools – spades, border spades, border forks, all those sort of things,' Garrett explains. 'But now and again you'll come up with an idea or you'll find something that really fills a certain niche for you. And the tickling fork has done that for me. Our borders are so tightly packed in with plants – and as with many borders you've got to really get in there amongst it and tickle the soil or work in a bit of compost or just do a bit of weeding or take your footprints out. And the fact that this has a long handle and a narrow head, it fits that need perfectly. It just makes it very easy for people to use. Initially to someone who hasn't used one it looks really awkward, but it fills a hole for us.'

The story of its discovery is as unlikely as it is entertaining. 'I came about it via a Welsh farmer who gave it to me. He was actually using it for poaching trout from the river, but he said he also found it useful for his potatoes. I hadn't seen a tool like it before. We're always on the lookout for good tools that can make our life easier, so it was a real "Bingo!" moment. I don't know where he got it from.'

Although it resembles a hand fork that's been attached to a long handle, it was evident on closer inspection that the tool was purpose-made: although for what purpose remains unclear. 'I was just having a short holiday in North Wales and I got talking to the farmer as he was fishing,' recalls Garrett. 'I helped him to pull his boat in and then we just got chatting. He was great, very warm and friendly. When I asked him about the fork he said, "I'm too old for veg gardening now, so you can use it". So he ended up giving me this fork and when I got back home I sent him some bulbs in return. It was a nice exchange.'

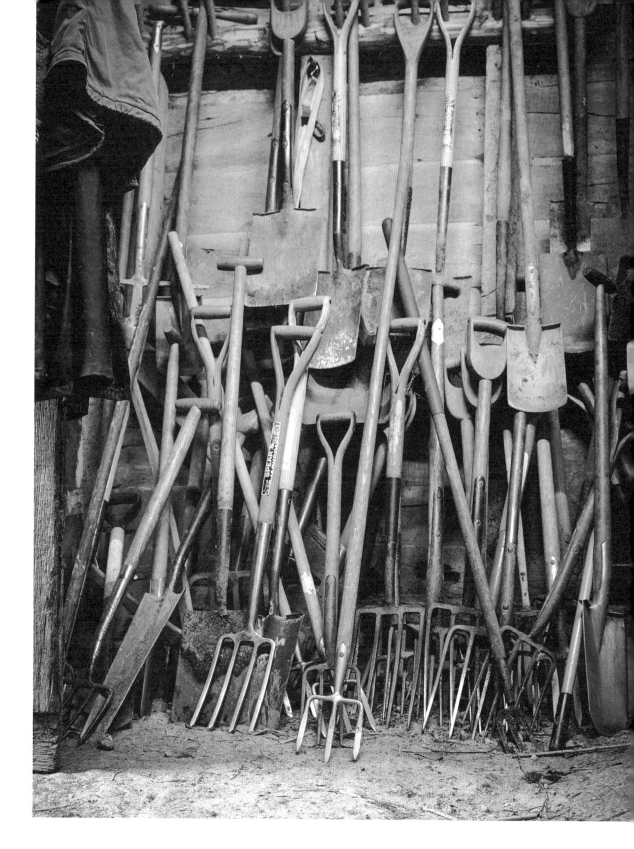

'I actually thought, this looks like a pretty useless tool… but you can stand upright to use it so it's great for otherwise back-breaking work… All the other gardeners wanted it'

In fact the 'bingo' moment didn't come until Garrett got the fork home and set to work with it. 'I actually thought, this looks like a pretty useless tool,' he admits, 'but I took it back to Dixter and found it so handy – you can stand upright to use it so it's great for otherwise back-breaking work. I use it for weeding… All the other gardeners wanted it. In fact they all started nicking it off me so I went to the local blacksmith to get more made. For whatever reason he couldn't do it, so we went to Sneeboer instead. And it's now a Dixter tool.' (Incidentally, the only reason Garrett mentions the blacksmith – besides stressing his initial intention to have it locally made – is, it transpires, to point out that the blacksmith still has his original fork: 'When I asked him where it was he said he couldn't find it!')

For those who don't know it, adding the Dixter name is something of a mark of authenticity in the horticultural world, revered as it is for its unique, easy charm. 'It's such a lovely, vibrant place,' enthuses Garrett. 'I think that's so important: there are loads of those stately home-type places, and some of them are like museums. It could easily be a place where they just process you through, take your money at the gate, you have a look and you go – but Dixter has this lovely organic, living feel about it. It's all about people. There's no real hierarchy – we've got kids who have been on the street mixing with university-educated kids and people who've worked at Kew… and all with the single purpose of making that place sing. And at the same time you've got 14-year-olds working with 90-year-olds, so there's that real community and passing down of knowledge.'

Garrett now sees the tickling fork as an indispensible component of the Dixter tool shed: an example perhaps of not realising what the real problem is until you discover the solution. And for Garrett, the problem in hand was generated by their preference for compost over mulch at Dixter. (In essence, while both add vital nutrients and organic materials to the soil, mulch suppresses seed germination as it is applied to the top of the soil as a protective layer: compost, on the other hand, is worked into the soil to reach the roots of the plants.)

'We want to put organic matter between the plants, but if we left it as a mulch we wouldn't be able to have any self-seeders,' explains Garrett. 'So all those plants like opium poppies wouldn't be able to germinate. So instead we throw compost on, but then we work that compost into the soil, and this tool is ideal for that. It's not a digging tool as such, you're not turning the borders over or using it for planting, you're just using it for working the top layer of soil and bringing some of that soil to the surface. It means we can still get the organic matter incorporated between the plants in those tight spaces without treading on the borders, because we can reach a long way with it. You're only pushing the prongs about an inch and a half into the soil, it's just a gentle action – tickling or fluffing up the soil. It's just a finishing-off tool. But certainly I wouldn't want to garden without it.'

'I came about it via a Welsh farmer who gave it to me. He was actually using it for poaching trout from the river, but he said he also found it useful for his potatoes… I took it back to Dixter and found it so handy… now it's a Dixter tool'

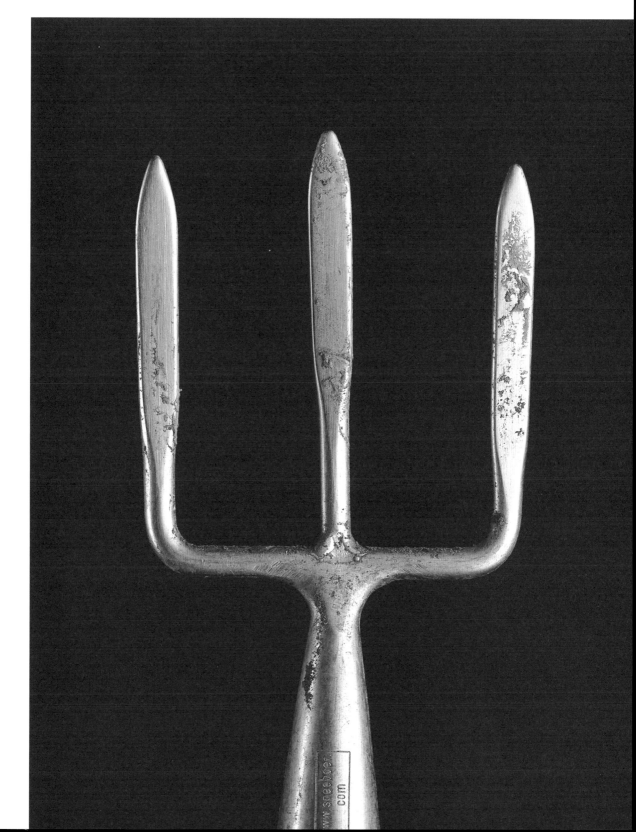

Collections 04:

Gardening

A set of garden implements used in the planting,
digging and management of gardens and parks,
courtesy of RHS Gardens.

Clockwise from far left: hand trowel; edging tools; two-pronged hand fork;
aerating tool; bamboo cane; bill hook; pin and line stake

The Onion Hoe
border agency

Set within the ruins of a manor house dating back to the Middle Ages in part, Sissinghurst Castle near Cranbrook in Kent is one of the most iconic gardens in England. It was made famous by Harold Nicolson and Vita Sackville-West, who bought the dilapidated site in the 1930s, and set about renovating it, producing an early and influential example of dividing garden space into various 'rooms' using high clipped hedges, brick walls and doorways.

The couple were both accomplished writers – Nicolson as a diarist, particularly throughout his time as a Member of Parliament, a period that spanned the Second World War; and Sackville-West as a novelist and gardening correspondent (she was also famously Virginia Woolf's lover). Sackville-West converted the Elizabethan Tower that stood at the centre of the grounds into her writing room, but it is the garden that was perhaps the couple's greatest – and most influential – legacy.

On first seeing what her son Nigel Nicolson described as 'the battered relic of an Elizabethan house in which not a single room was habitable'*, its 'future garden a rubbish dump'*, Sackville-West announced 'I think we shall be very happy here… I think we can make something rather lovely out of it.'* Their planting was revolutionary – letting plants stray over paths ('they must not be cut back, the visitor must duck'*), allowing parts of the garden to lie fallow as nature required, using the remains of a moat to frame the garden and creating their famously iridescent White Garden as one of the many 'rooms'.

Today, Sissinghurst is equally famous among gardeners for a tool with which it has become synonymous: the onion hoe. It has, current head gardener Troy Scott Smith admits, become something of a trademark among staff. 'I've worked here twice,' he says; 'first as a gardener from 1992–97, so I was introduced to the onion hoe back then, and when I left Sissinghurst I continued to use one, whatever garden I've worked in. It was so nice to come back to Sissinghurst as head gardener to find that everyone is still using onion hoes. I even found my original one that I used to use: I still recognised it!'

In her final years, Sackville-West handed over the upkeep of the garden to head gardeners Pam Schwerdt and Sibylle Kreutzberger. 'Most of our gardening techniques and tools really stem from Pam and Sibylle,' he says. 'They were here for 30 years, and I wouldn't be surprised if the onion hoe came from them – but equally so Vita might have introduced it – there are certainly pictures of her with a Sussex trug, and the two tend to go hand-in-hand here.'

The particular tool that Scott Smith once used is now only good for a museum piece – so instead we've photographed an example that he still uses: a modern design by the Dutch company Sneeboer. 'It just feels nicely balanced.'

The popularity of the onion hoe among the Sissinghurst garden team is chiefly down to its versatility. Held in one hand, with a curved neck that allows one to reach between closely grown plants, it derives its name from its traditional use of weeding between onions. 'It's all about the detail,' says Scott Smith. 'We leave things to sow seed within the borders here, and so it can be a little bit heavy handed to use anything else. The nature of an onion hoe means you have to get down to use it. You don't sit or kneel: you crouch, bending your knees and back, using it in that style. It means your head's really low and you can see underneath the skirts of the perennials and lift them up to check for pests and disease; or to see if there are slugs sitting there. You can choose very accurately which seedlings to leave to develop and then hoe the other ones off. You're so much more in control than you are standing up with a long hoe.'

As Scott Smith has already alluded to, the onion hoe tends to be used in conjunction with an old-fashioned Sussex trug, made from hazel and chestnut. 'The two go pretty much together, almost as a single tool,' he says. 'The great thing about the onion hoe is, due to the shape of the head, you can reach over and pick up the handle of the trug with it, which is really useful if you have your hands full. You can also reach across perennials – you don't have to stand in them – and then you can hook out your trug with the weeds in from there.'

A sturdy and reliable tool, it can be used for heavier digging work than simply weeding too. 'They're pretty strong, so you can dig out clumping perennials – in other words not ones with a tap root – but they're robust enough to stab into the soil and actually dig out a plant. And also I use mine quite a lot for actually leaning on. Our soil is a heavy clay soil at Sissinghurst, so you want to stay off it as much as possible – and if I can lean on my onion hoe and reach in to do a task with my other hand, all the better.'

What makes the onion hoe truly indispensible to the team at Sissinghurst, in fact, is this very flexibility of use and role. 'I often only need this one tool,' says Scott Smith. 'I don't need a trowel or anything else. You can do quite a lot of vital jobs with just the one tool, which is what makes it so handy.'

Portrait of a Marriage by Nigel Nicolson (Weidenfeld & Nicolson, 1973)

The Vernier Caliper
measure for measure

While versatility of use and adaptability can be a virtue in many tools – allowing for that ability to improvise, both in terms of design and also in the use of the tool itself – some tools are so precise, exact and clearly defined that they allow for no leeway or margin for error. And when the end result is to accurately measure time, the accuracy of the making is imperative.

In horology, the ultimate challenge is to build a mechanical clock capable of keeping time to within one second over a span of 100 days – a definition laid down by the great 18th-century British clockmaker John Harrison. Although he died without ever achieving this feat, Harrison did leave behind plans for a clock that he thought would be capable of it. More than 200 years after his death, subsequent work by Martin Burgess and – later – Donald Saff, working to Harrison's original specifications, resulted in a clock that lost only 5/8 of a second over 200 days – still regarded as 'the most accurate mechanical clock with a pendulum swinging in free air'.

Still considered the Holy Grail of clockmakers, it's a goal that occupies Jake Sutton for a large proportion of his waking hours – supplemented by his work as an artist, set designer, inventor of various contraptions (he is a member of the Society of Model and Experimental Makers) and an award-winning toolmaker. And he thinks he might be getting there. 'In clockmaking it's either right or it's wrong,' states Sutton. 'There's no in between. It either fits or it doesn't. That's absolutely essential.' For him, then, the ultimate tool is one that can eliminate the inaccuracies that plague his craft.

Made more than 40 years ago by Moore & Wright (one of the most revered English companies when it comes to making precision tools), to say Sutton's Vernier caliper is invaluable is something of an understatement. 'I'm handling it virtually all day,' he says. 'Everything I make, I check for size using it. It's like your second hand really. It's the everyday tool of the trade: it has the ability to measure either the internal dimensions – ie how big a hole is, or external – how thick something is. You can measure a human hair with it (I've not got much of that to measure myself!) – or it can tell you how thick a piece of paper is.'

Appropriately for the world in which Sutton operates, the Vernier caliper is in itself something of an anachronism, utilising as it does a Vernier scale – a visual aid that allows one to read differing degrees of graduation, providing a more precise measurement than a uniform scale (as found on a ruler, for instance). 'Nowadays if you went into a shop they'd sell you a digital one,' says Sutton. 'It is old-fashioned, but it's what you grow up with really. I've tried digital ones, but the battery runs out…'

Having first closed up the caliper and zeroed the dial, the caliper has the ability to measure to a thousandth of an inch or a hundredth of a millimetre, moving along each dial in turn to give you the next decimal place. 'What you can do is, if you want to use it as a comparator – you might have 10 objects and you want to check if they are all exactly the same – you can put the piece between the measuring faces of the caliper and rotate the dial so that the pointer is on zero. And you can very quickly click each piece in, close it, and the indicator will then show you by how many thousandths of an inch they differ.'

The ability to compare the thicknesses or lengths of component parts in clockmaking is the basis of all else that follows. 'You can't make anything unless you know the dimensions of it,' says Sutton. Which might seem obvious, but Sutton is working to such an infinitesimal scale in his work that knowing the precise size of anything is impossible without being able to measure it yourself. 'I make everything in my clocks – every shaft, every wheel is made from bare metal,' he explains. 'But when you buy metal and it's supposed to be, say, a quarter of an inch round, it never is. It's always a couple of thousandths out either way. And you need to know that. You need to understand what it is you've bought and compensate for the actual thickness of the sheet.'

In short, the parts need to fit together, or it won't work. 'So if you have a hole a certain size, you know the shaft going into it has to be a certain size – and you can then machine them to fit. So if you want something to be 88 thousandths of an inch in diameter, I can arrange that on the machine tools.'

Having said all this, Sutton then points out with a wry laugh that a lot of the dimensions in the design itself aren't all that important. 'You have a scheme and obviously you've calculated the gear reductions and the teeth and all the rest of it, but it's not like a CAD drawing – the actual distance between the centres to make two gears mesh doesn't actually matter: it's the fact that the gears run well together. So that's the difference between precision engineering in a car, say, where it has to be done exactly according to the drawing. With a clock you're making something quite organic, because it's put together so that all the pieces relate together and work smoothly.'

The frustrations of the job lie in its very nature: 'It's the fact that if it's not right it's wrong: every single thing has to be absolutely right.' That said, Sutton remarks that the regulator he's currently calibrating is keeping time in line with John Harrison's own record. 'Believe it or not I think I'm actually getting there! But to get to that point you have to consider absolutely everything – even down to the thickness of the oils, which can slow them down. The case has to be screwed firmly to the wall: there's so many variables. Even opening the door – the pendulum is paddling the air inside the case, and there's a degree of air resistance around it. When you open the door, the restriction to the pendulum is slightly less because there's more air, it's freer – so the air is effectively lighter.'

But Sutton points out that he also works to a highly therapeutic rhythm. 'The beauty of a clock is – with a regulator that has a one-second pendulum – the tick is that of a very slow heartbeat. And that is why it is such a relaxing thing to have in a room: it's the pulse of the room really. Your heart rate tends to tune into that, so it is very calming. I have a clock that came off the bridge of a wartime aircraft carrier and it's got a very urgent tick. Because you're using it to look out for the flash of guns and waiting for the shell to land, the second finger is absolutely the most important thing about the clock. It's a lovely clock, I have it in the workshop. But I can't wind it up because the tick makes you nervous. It's the very opposite of the one-second tick. But I suppose if you're on the bridge of an aircraft carrier it's probably not a bad thing to be kept on edge. If you had a second regulator everyone would be nodding off!'

In fact, he's so relaxed he cheerfully admits the whole process is ultimately futile. 'The interesting thing is, for all that effort, we don't actually need a clock that's so accurate! You can just look at your computer, or the atomic clocks that run the world. So you don't need it, but there's something beautiful about it – it's like a living thing.'

'It is old-fashioned… I've tried digital ones, but the battery runs out'

The Widger
seed capital

Many of the tools featured in this book are priceless. Some have been passed down through generations, or are antiques that have been actively sought out. Others have to be lovingly and painstakingly maintained. And then there's the widger. Looking like nothing more than an old-fashioned tent peg, this unassuming piece of shiny, bent metal is, nonetheless, an invaluable part of the horticulturalist's toolbelt.

Invaluable maybe; but certainly not priceless. 'You can get them online for under £5,' says Emma Davies, owner of the Walled Nursery in Tongswood, Kent, a magnificent walled garden consisting of a total of 13 Victorian glasshouses – a site she bought with her husband and business partner Monty Davies (a landscape gardener) in 2010, a full 20 years after they first set their eyes on it. Davies has certainly done her apprenticeship in the gardening world, having previously worked at both Great Dixter and Sissinghurst, two of the most famous gardens in England (and both featured elsewhere on these pages). With more than 20 years' hands-on experience, she prides herself that the Walled Nursery does its own propagation, growing 80 per cent of its plants from seed or cuttings on site.

'I studied commercial horticulture at college and I've been propagating for 20-plus years, but I'm relatively new to the widger – I wasn't aware of it until this past year – and I think it's a much, much better tool than the alternatives,' she says. Davies was belatedly introduced to the widger by a retired propagation expert who she describes as her 'growing mentor'. 'She gave this tool to me, and just said, "This is a widger, it's the best tool to use". And I totally agree with her now.'

A spatula-like instrument made from durable stainless steel, the widger has many uses, including pricking out and transplanting seedlings, loosening soil and applying fertiliser. Like many tools found in horticulture, the name itself sounds completely made up – which it most likely is. Not to be confused with a dibber – a pen-like tool used for making holes for seed sowing – the name seems to perfectly describe a non-existent verb to match its use. (Incidentally, the widger sometimes comes with a small dibber on its opposite end – or even a two-pronged fork.)

But there is a vital side to all this widging and dibbing. The Walled Nursery is dedicated to ensuring guaranteed provenance for everything it grows, as well as the preservation of the historic glasshouses, built by Foster & Pearson

'You could be using it all day, so it's very comfortable
to use. It's like a big shoehorn really'

Ltd of Nottingham – who were renowned for their horticultural structures, including several commissions by Queen Victoria – in the late 1800s. (A generous donation from the granddaughter of Ernest Hardcastle, the original head gardener at Tongswood from 1914 to 1945, has helped make this a reality.)

Before the widger came into her life, Davies used thin bamboo cane ('the sort of thing you'd use to stake small plants, with a pointy edge'). 'We sow by seed and then take cuttings – and we then prick out all of those into what we call a pan, and we let them grow in the pan until they're a good enough size to be transplanted into a 7cm pot,' she explains. 'It's really important for us that the plants don't have too big a jump up in the amount of compost they're growing in. Using a widger, the reason you've got that groove in it is you can get a good root ball around the seedling, so it minimises any damage to the roots.'

The widger enables you to scoop under the delicate roots and push them up from below, rather than them being pulled from above. 'You're not cutting the root because it hasn't got sharp sides, so you can go all the way around the plant and then lift it out,' says Davies. 'And we actually hold the seedling on the end of the widger and transplant it over to the pot like that, because the less you touch it with your hands, the less you damage it.'

The subtle dents in the profile of the widger are there by design, rather than being signs of wear. 'That's just for comfort. You could be using it all day, so it's very comfortable to use. It's like a big shoehorn really,' says Davies. 'We have it with us all the time now, in our pouches, so you use it for all kinds of things. You can go quite deep into a pot with it – we don't use huge pot sizes, we tend to keep them to one litre, no bigger than that. So if you walk past a plant and you can see it's raised itself up, which can happen, you can use the widger to dig it from underneath and get it back down to the right position.'

For a new discovery, the impression you get of the widger is that it is the sort of tool you'd expect to see hundreds of scattered around the garden, rusty and covered in clumps of soil. 'Well there will be now,' says Davies. 'The majority of the tools we use are rusty and old. These are only shiny because we haven't had them that long!'

'The less you touch the seedling with your hands, the less you damage it'

Collections 05:

Glass Making

A set of tools for holding, shaping, blowing
and cutting glass, as used by Peter Layton,
founder of London Glassblowing.

Clockwise from top left: wooden block; caliper; diamond shears; straight
shears; tweezers; taglia; jacks; trim shears

The Turning Tool
too much chatter can be good

The importance of the tool to its maker can often extend beyond its functionality – gaining emotional weight and depth via its connections to other makers, previous generations or its particular history.

'Despite coming from Japan and sounding fairly exotic, my turning tool is actually quite rudimentary in some ways,' says the award-winning contemporary ceramicist and designer Billy Lloyd. 'This one will wear away and one day it will be of no use to me – because it will be too small from being so worn. But it's got a few years left in it still. And then it will prove a good blueprint to make another of the same kind.'

Essentially a carving tool made from mild steel, the turning tool is a basic piece of potter's kit – used, as the names suggests, during turning (the stage in pottery that follows the throwing of a piece, in which the rough design and shape is refined). The reason the particular tool pictured here has resonance for Lloyd is that it was originally a gift from the potter Lisa Hammond MBE, for whom he apprenticed having completed his BA in Ceramics at Camberwell College of Arts. 'I worked with her for a year at Maze Hill pottery in London,' says Lloyd, 'and at some point she went to Japan and came back with a small handful of tools for me – of which this was one. She bought it from a pretty legendary shop there called Tokyu Hands.'

Besides being a useful and efficient tool for a part of the job at which he excels, it also speaks to him of a complex relationship and the starting point of his career. 'I wasn't a fantastic thrower at that stage,' he admits. 'At Camberwell I'd been combining throwing with hand building – I wasn't making functional pottery, that's for sure. Whereas Lisa's pottery at Maze Hill is built on the foundations of everyday tableware. So part of my role was to learn how to throw the standard ware that she produces. That's what every apprentice does. My job was to look after the maintenance of the studio, assist Lisa with day-to-day tasks, preparing clay – she's well known for soda firing, which is similar to salt firing – it takes 24 hours.'

Lloyd sees his time at Maze Hill as a pivotal moment in his career – in some ways because he realised it was heading in the wrong direction for him, and is honest and open enough to admit that. 'I got on very well with Lisa and it was an enjoyable time, but I only spent one year there, which is a comparatively short time. Although it was a great learning experience, I don't think we were a great match in terms of style. My work is very different. I have total respect for what Lisa makes and how she does it, but for some reason we didn't quite click in terms of the work. But I came away with this lovely tool – and that was given to me by Lisa. I take great pleasure in using it. It takes me back to Maze Hill pottery and it gets my head out of the studio in some ways because it was fabricated in Japan, which is somewhere I have only just recently visited. It gets me thinking about more than just the function it's designed to be used for.'

What he also discovered, via this gifted tool, was a passion for turning. 'Turning is the stage in pottery where, once you've thrown a batch of pots on a wheel, you then leave them to dry – not bone dry but what they call 'leather hard' – or maybe a bit before that, so there's still water content: it's still moist,'

'When I first started using it, I liked the texture that the chattering produced, so I would accentuate it by using the tool in the wrong way'

he explains. 'And then you put the pot back on the wheel, upside down, and you can start to refine the exterior of the pot. You can emphasise the curves if it's a curved bowl, or straighten out the outside line if it's a straight-sided beaker. And you can put things like a foot ring on – which you'll find on the underside of most pieces of crockery.'

'So it's a tool that helps you refine the form, after you've thrown it. And for me, certainly once I found my creative voice, turning was the aspect that I've always really enjoyed. The throwing was a means to creating a vessel, but the turning was the point at which I could really refine the shape, and I've always been very interested in the small details such as foot rings which are often overlooked by the end user, but they are really vital aspects of the pot.'

So this tool allowed Lloyd to express his versatility as a designer – and played a vital role in making decisions about his career and – as he puts it – 'what I wanted things to look like'.

As it's made of mild steel, the turning tool has a tendency to go soft and rusty if not maintained. 'Clay is actually quite an aggressive material,' he says. 'It's pretty coarse – even fine porcelain. If you're using a grogged clay [which has a high percentage of silica and alumina], as Lisa does, then it will blunt a lot quicker. But if you keep it sharp, it's perfect. There's two different sized blades to it: a smaller one and a larger one. So it just depends how much surface you want to carve at the same time: the smaller one is good for doing the foot rings on mugs, and the large blade is better for the exterior wall of a piece, where you have to cover a bit more ground at once. And it's got a really nice balance to it, so you can just twist it round if you want to use the other end easily enough.'

One final, special characteristic of Lloyd's turning tool dates back to the days when he was still learning his craft. 'If you don't use this tool properly you'll get a lot of chattering, which is the sort of rippling effect you can see when the blade stutters on the surface. When I first started using it, I liked the texture that the chattering produced, so I would accentuate it by using the tool in the wrong way, but creating what I wanted to create from it. So depending on how you use the tool, you can inadvertently create a texture on the piece that you're working on. And you have to learn to use it properly to avoid that. You make it right by doing it wrong in the first place, and learning how to correct it from there. So really it's not a mistake – it's all part of the process.'

'It's a tool that helps you refine the form, after you've thrown it. Once I found my creative voice, turning was the aspect that I've always really enjoyed'

Material, Cloth and Decoration

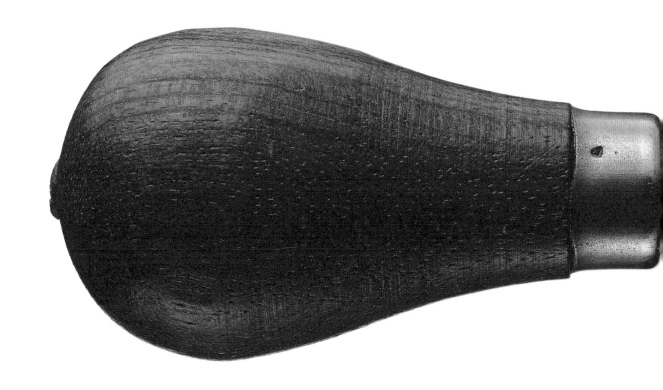

The Bradawl

making a point

A small, pointed hand tool with a bulbous handle, the bradawl is principally used in woodwork for making indentations in surfaces before inserting a nail or screw. Not only does this create a 'biting point' for the screw or nail, it also prevents splitting across the grain. The suffix 'awl' links it to a number of similar spiked tools, including a stitch awl (for piercing holes in leather) and a scratch awl (for scribing a line in wood, to be followed by a chisel or handsaw).

As with many tools, the bradawl has also been appropriated by another trade for a secondary purpose: it is commonly found in dressmaking and tailoring, where it is used for puncturing or piercing patterns in order to mark them precisely. But there is a third use that is possibly unique to the artist Zoe Bradley, who specialises in paper as a medium across many disciplines – combining fashion, display and theatre in her bespoke installations.

Having trained in fashion design and apprenticed for Alexander McQueen, Bradley's creation of experimental hand-pleated showpieces for the Japanese fashion designer Michiko Koshino's A/W2005 catwalk show proved pivotal in her move into paper sculpture, gaining her a commission from Liberty. She has since become the go-to artist in her field for global brands including Louis Vuitton, Smythson and Christian Louboutin.

And in her sideways career change from fashion designer into paper artist, she took one key tool with her: the bradawl. Rather than using it to puncture holes with, Bradley uses the tool in an entirely unique way. 'When I studied fashion design, both at university and college, I'd had some use of the bradawl,' she says. 'And when I started working specifically in paper, because I still had my dressmaking equipment, I just picked it up. As I developed my work in paper, I found a different use for it – for curling the edges of paper, scratching score lines… and now it's become almost like a pencil to me, the way I use it.'

Acknowledging the unavoidable similarity between her surname and the name of her tool of choice, Bradley notes that she does share a family connection with tailoring. 'My great grandfather was a tailor, and I remember my dad saying, "Gosh you really remind me of him" – even of the way he'd sit. Dad would tell stories of him sitting cross-legged on the side of the pattern-cutting table, like I do.' Bradley's initial choice of career dovetails neatly here – and, she remarks, as with the precise techniques of tailoring, her work is very much focused on hand-forming designs.

'The great thing about the bradawl is that it's a tiny bit of kit. It's so small you can fit it in a pencil case, which makes it really accessible and useful – although it's probably not the best thing to put in your handbag,' says Bradley. 'It's also the one bit of kit that, if I didn't have it with me, I couldn't do the job. It's almost like a sewing machine: it's my tool to connect and translate what I do.'

In her signature oversized paper flower designs, Bradley uses the bradawl to 'finish' the edges; producing a lifelike curl to the petals and stamen. She will also use it to create texture – for instance in one of her large exhibition pieces for Sotheby's, in which she created the impression of silk by scoring multiple lines on the surface of countless sheets of metallic paper. And, finally, she will use it for scoring – both in order to fold paper and also to mark it in the manner of a pencil line.

And then, of course, there's the job for which it was intended. 'Obviously, if you need to make a hole in something, it's ideal for that, because that's its original purpose,' says Bradley. 'But I use it more often for scoring the top surface of the paper.' There is a particular technique that Bradley has developed for this in order to make it most effective: 'You have to use it at a specific angle – to get it almost flat against the paper, because what you want is a fine dented line, not a cut-through line.'

The tool has become something of a trademark for Bradley – not only something she will always travel with, but something she has introduced into her team's standard kit. 'I train everyone who works with me in how to use it now – we never put any pencil lines on paper at all. Initially, when I first started working in paper, everything was hand cut, whereas now everything is illustrated, artworked and laser cut. So there was no longer any need to work in pencil and have those dirty, smudgy lines. It was about needing to score something and leave a line, but for that to be almost invisible.'

There is nothing precious about the way Bradley uses the tool – she laughs at the idea of having a favourite, noting that she will have 10 or 20 in the studio at any one time – 'and everyone uses them, so they're quite interchangeable'.

A tool, then, born of necessity – that has now become necessity in itself. 'If I'm on a job or a photoshoot, or at a particular location and I haven't got one to hand when I'm trying to finish something, I'll try to do the same thing with a pencil or a pair of scissors, but it's not the same,' says Bradley. 'It's the technique of it, it becomes like automatic pilot – an extension of your hands. It's a weird thing, but I couldn't go without it now.'

The Pestle and Mortar
mix and match

The pestle and mortar is one of the earliest existing hand-shaped tools known to have been used by man. Examples have been found dating back to 35,000BC, and the name derives from the Latin *pistillum* (a pounding instrument) and *mortarium* (a receptacle for pounding). Not much seems to have changed in the intervening years in terms of design, and most cultures seem to have developed their own, very similar versions – early examples can be found everywhere from Indian to Mayan communities.

The mortar is commonly made of a hard rock such as granite or basalt, while the pestle can be stone or wood. The modern Wedgwood mortar and pestle, which first came into use in the Western world in 1759 for pharmaceutical use, is made of a porcelain mortar and a wooden pestle tipped with porcelain at the head. It is traditionally linked with medicine and the grinding of natural materials to produce powders – although in modern usage it tends to be a kitchen utensil, used for mixing ingredients and producing pastes for cooking, or for grinding spices into powder – as well as husking and dehulling grain.

For Pedro da Costa Felgueiras, a world-renowned paint, lacquer and pigment expert who runs Lacquer Studios, the pestle and mortar is crucial for his work. 'I use it almost every day,' he says. 'I do not buy any ready-made paints, so it is an essential tool in the making of all my colours: be it for historic houses or newly designed pieces.'

To say he doesn't buy ready-made paints is something of an understatement: a large part of da Costa Felgueiras' work involves restoration projects that require not simply colour-matching but process-matching. In other words, if a historic house he is working on was originally painted with blue verditer distemper, he will recreate the colour using the original techniques: slaking the dry pigment in water overnight, grinding and mixing it with rabbit-skin glue. (In this particular case, it also needs to be kept warm and stirred constantly to render it liquid and applied to the wall very rapidly – meaning he will often work through the night.)

He will mix pigments and make paint using a large, acid-proof, ceramic, laboratory pestle and mortar – such as the one pictured on these pages, which is ideal because 'it's big, it's old, and it has years of patina from using it for over two decades. The interior is also smooth from its long-term use, which I think helps in the making of a better paint.'

'I do not buy any ready-made paints, so it is an essential tool in the making of all my colours'

BRUSHES

VERY IMPORTANT

1 — WASH IN WHITE SPIRIT
(POT ON THE LEFT HANDSIDE)
BE CAREFULL TO USE ONLY THE
TOP PART AND DO NOT DISTURBE DREGS —
YOU CAN DE CANT IT INTO THE PAINT
KETTLE

2 — WITTH BOILING WATER WASH BRUSHES
WITH FAIRY LIQUID.
USE THE SCRUBING BRUSH TO START
TAKING THE PAINT CLOSER TO THE
HANDLE — VERY IMPORTANT!

3 — ~~THOROUGH~~ WASH BRUSHES WITH BIG
OLIVE OIL CUBE OF SOAP. MASSAGE
HAIR VERY WELL, UNTIL THERE IS
NO COLOUR COMING OUT!

4 — FINALY — SQUEEZE HAIR FLAT AND FORM

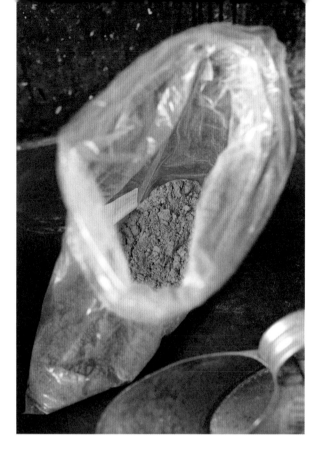

'Every pigment reacts differently, so it is not so much about the tool itself as the conjunction of the pestle and mortar and the medium… For example, if you grind lapis lazuli for too long, instead of a vibrant deep blue, you get a murky grey colour'

While some tools can take years to perfect, the pestle and mortar is such a simple, ancient and intuitive set of implements that it is the material it is used with that demands technical knowledge and understanding. 'Every pigment reacts differently,' says da Costa Felgueiras. 'So it is not so much about the tool itself as the conjunction of the pestle and mortar, and the medium: the pigments used and the strain required to make good paint. The skill is more about knowing which pigments to use, with the right media and knowhow. For example, if you grind lapis lazuli for too long, instead of a vibrant deep blue, you get a murky grey colour.'

For da Costa Felgueiras, this process is often instinctual and even hypnotic. 'I can almost get into a trance,' he says, 'as the beating of the pestle hitting on the mortar makes a sound akin to a gong in a Buddhist temple: thus putting me into a state of semi-meditation.' While the majority of the grinding work is done using a pestle and mortar, he will use other kitchen utensils to initially mix and crush the pigment at the outset of the paint-making process.

However committed he is to using the pestle and mortar for historical accuracy and its effectiveness, da Costa Felgueiras admits there can be distinct disadvantages too. 'It can be quite heavy,' he says, 'especially if it is full of lead paint.' It can also be impractical simply because of the scale of work he is required to carry out. 'Sometimes it's not big enough to make large batches of paint – especially when you are undertaking a project in one of the grand historic houses in Britain, and so you are obliged to repeat the process many times over. On the other hand, if I had a big industrial machine to make lead paint I would not be able to use it now, due to health and safety requirements. So, the challenge of using it is actually what makes it possible for me to still be able to provide lead paint for historic buildings.' Indeed, most large manufacturers have now stopped supplying it for this reason – meaning the old-fashioned process is the only way to produce the paint required.

Of course, there is another drawback in not buying your paint pre-mixed in a tin: 'Quite a bit of elbow grease is necessary in order to make it this way!'

'It's big, it's old, and it has years of patina from using it for over two decades. The interior is also smooth from its long-term use, which I think helps in the making of a better paint'

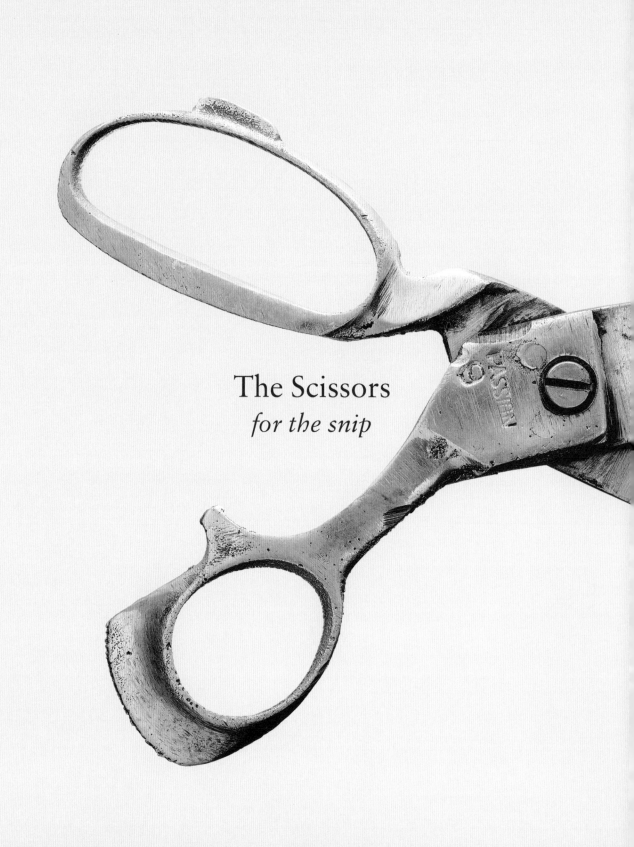

The Scissors
for the snip

A pair of scissors is perhaps the ultimate example of a tool that has become so ubiquitous and all-purpose that it is often overlooked – or is regarded simply as a household implement rather than being considered a tool per se.

Indeed the word 'scissors' itself is used for a catch-all that covers a multitude of specific tools and uses – from dressmaking to carpet making – and will differ vastly from the classic orange-handled Fiskars style (which can rightly claim to be the world's most popular scissors, with over a billion pairs sold since their launch in 1967). The essential design, however – of a pair of opposing blades joined so that they could be squeezed together to produce a cutting edge – dates back a little further: to Ancient Mesopotamia circa 2,000BC, to be exact.

These early specimens were in fact closer in construction to traditional blade shears or glass jacks, with a flexible strip of metal at the base joining the two blades, and are known as spring scissors. A more recognisable scissor shape, with the blades joined by a pivot in front of the handles, emerged in Rome in AD100 – although similar styles also developed independently in China, Korea and Japan.

A couple of millennia later, and the basic shape remains largely unchanged. 'Scissors are one of the most familiar and well-used household objects, yet when it comes to using them in my practice, the subtleties and quality of them as a tool to carry out specific tasks has given me the greatest respect for the craftsmanship that goes into the making of a good pair,' says Abigail Booth of Forest + Found, a creative partnership she founded in 2014 with fellow artist Max Bainbridge. Working with traditional methods of craft to produce sculptural wooden objects and large textile pieces, their focus is on the use of hand tools in particular and the direct experience of handcrafting an object. This, coupled with their ability to demonstrate a contemporary relevance to traditional skills – not to mention their photogenic, social media-friendly profiles – has put them at the centre of the current revival for the principles and mores of craftsmanship.

Not least, for Booth this means a working practice that makes having a pair of scissors at hand a daily essential. 'My work is about construction and the manipulation of cloth through intricate and sometimes quite brutal patchwork techniques,' she explains. 'This process requires the ability to break down cloth into individually shaped pieces to be remade, cut into and pieced back together again – so the ability to accurately wield a good pair of scissors is crucial.'

'Everything from the balance and the weight of a pair [of scissors] in your hand is crucial to the ease and efficiency of carrying out different tasks'

For someone with such specialised demands – and working in various media and materials – there is no single pair of scissors that will suffice for every job. 'I have six pairs in total and each one is completely different – and set aside for unique and individual tasks when working in my studio.' But when it comes to maintenance and upkeep, each pair demands the same attention and care. 'Key to all of them is the quality of the steel and the sharpness of the blades,' says Booth. 'I look for this across the board, whether I am using large fabric shears to rip down lengths of fabric, a more traditional set of tailor's scissors for accurate cutting of cloth, or my tiny but precise stork snips to cut thread as I hand stitch.'

Choosing the right pair for the job often comes down to a personal preference for what feels right in the hand. 'Everything from the balance and the weight of a pair in your hand is crucial to the ease and efficiency of carrying out different tasks,' says Booth. 'Each pair I own has been acquired over time – and quickly they become an old friend as they become integral to certain parts of my making process.'

Even within very similar tasks, individual demands of the job will necessitate the ability to call on subtle differences between tools. For instance, Booth notes how she owns two pairs of stork snips from Ernest Wright & Sons (now sadly closed down), each varying slightly in the length of the blades and the size of the 'bows' (or handles)... 'And yet these differences allow each pair to fulfill two very different roles,' she says. 'One pair is so nimble and sharp that I can cut thread as I stitch incredibly fast – so as not to disrupt my rhythm of working – and the other are slightly blunter and shorter in the blade, so that I can hold them backwards and pointed towards myself in order to accurately in-cut curved seams for hand-stitching and appliqué.'

Thus, picking one specific example to photograph as the epitome of its type becomes an almost impossible ask. While Booth couldn't part with the pair of steel tailor's scissors from Cloth House shown here (used for cutting cloth), neither could she do without any of the other pairs in her collection. 'The need for dexterity and sleight of hand is so important for the precision I am trying to achieve while working in cloth,' she says, 'that my collection of scissors has become indispensable for producing the character of line that I am striving to achieve in my work.'

'Each pair I own has been acquired over time – and quickly they become an old friend as they become integral to certain parts of my making process'

Collections 06:

_____

Upholstery

A selection of implements used for cutting,
pinning, stretching, treating and tacking upholstery,
courtesy of Christopher Howe of Howe London

Clockwise from bottom left: fabric scissors; bent nose pliers/leather stretcher;
assorted needles – including curved needles and mattress needles; tack
hammer; tack remover; nail pull; beeswax; pliers; eyelet pliers

The Leather Hammer
creativity on tap

There are five principal leatherworking tools that all leather makers tend to have as their basic kit. These are the knife; the bone folder; the awl; an edged tool of some description; and the hammer.

'The hammer is used across all aspects of leather making, from when you fold and crease materials to when you're flattening your seams, to moulding around corners, and hammering the threads after you've stitched them in order to set them,' says Bill Amberg. One of the most respected names in British leathercraft, Amberg has more than 35 years' experience in the trade, his design projects varying enormously in scale – from wallets to architectural interiors (including the Leathersellers' Hall in the City of London). And he never goes anywhere without his hammer.

'It's used extensively,' he says. 'It's one of the key instruments of a leatherworker. And what's interesting about them is every nation's leatherworkers have a different hammer. So if you go to Spain, they're all using a wooden hammer that's held close in the hand; in France they have a much more elegant, long-shaped hammer; in England we have something that you hold in your fist, like two heads of a hammer but set in cast iron for you to hold, but we also have the more traditional-looking, flat-shaped hammer.'

Despite the locally flavoured nuances and individual design quirks, all leather hammers have a slightly enlarged, rounded head, which is highly polished because, instead of hammering nails, they are used for 'tapping' – a very different action. 'If you go to a leather factory, all you hear is this constant "tap-tap-tap"; it's not hammering as such,' says Amberg. Tapping is a way to produce a completely even, smooth edge and to remove creases – for instance where leather is folded over onto itself in a wallet. The smooth, rounded face can also be used in a circular motion, rubbing away blemishes 'in the way that you polish your boots with a spoon'. The bone folder – which is typically made from a beef rib – is also used for the same purpose. 'They're the unsung heroes of leatherwork,' Amberg enthuses. 'The sexy tool is obviously the knife, but actually the cool tools are the hammer and the bone folder.'

While some tools are specific to certain trades within the leather industry, the hammer is a universal tool across all the various vocations involved in the material – from bookbinders to saddlers, casemakers, cordwainers, curriers, girdlers, glovers and more. The particular hammer pictured here is Amberg's own personal tool – a vintage specimen that speaks of the leather trade and

'The sexy tool [for leatherworking] is obviously the knife, but the cool tools are the hammer and the bone folder'

bears the scars and wear earned through generations of use. He picked it up in 1984, when he first started in the leather trade and was trying to assemble his toolkit of five key pieces as detailed above – the equipment that could make up his standard repertoire for leather making.

'It came from my father's old cobbler in Northampton – where he and his family had had their shoes repaired forever – and who was retiring,' says Amberg. 'The bone folder I use is also from the same cobbler. So that means it's been in continuous leatherwork – not just from 35-odd years ago, when I started in 1984 – but the cobbler was still working until he was 70, so presumably he'd been using the hammer for 50 years or so. In other words it's been in the hands of leatherworkers for 80-plus years. It's a bit gnarly, it's not a perfect hammer, but it fits in my hand so well and it does everything that I need it to do. And even though it's got some burnished and cowled edges, I know where all its scratches and idiosyncrasies are.'

One such idiosyncrasy is a distinct crack in the head, which would usually rule it out as a viable tool, since the rounded head needs to be polished and maintained to protect the grain of the leather. Any impurities such as glue must also be cleaned from the face to prevent contamination – if a dirty hammer is used on the leather it can mark it permanently, rendering it unusable. 'You're only supposed to be creasing or flattening the leather,' explains Amberg. 'Hence that very domed and enlarged head. When they're new, they're obviously crisper than this one, but I love the fact that it's been tapping away for 80 years.'

The domed shape also helps to prevent 'edging' – catching the edge of the leather – which can happen with a traditional nail hammer's sharper profile. In simple terms, the purpose of a leather hammer is to spread the force of the blow to create an even surface, in contrast to most hammers, which are principally designed to focus the force to a fine point in order to maximise the power of the blow. This highlights one of the aspects of leatherwork that appeals to Amberg: 'Leather is lovely material to work with. It's really sympathetic in the hand, it's got a great feel, it's very malleable and it's *kind*. I do metalwork and woodwork on various jobs, and with metal, it's brutal – you've got to really attack it to do things. You don't have that with leather.'

The short length of the leather hammer also makes it very controllable and is ideal for the tapping technique. (Indeed other makers will often hold their hammers further up the handle if they are doing delicate work that requires more control.)

It's significant that Amberg has used the same hammer for 35 years and that the sense of history and provenance behind it is important to him. Whereas some makers can be more prosaic over individual tools, rejecting anything they see as 'sentimentality', Amberg encourages his staff to treasure and value their tools as unique to them, to be shaped by their work, just as the tools – and the work – shapes the maker. 'You tend to have one hammer that you stick with,' he says. 'When they first start here, all my workers make a leather roll, which is their tool roll, and they will all have a hammer of some sort. And they're expected to look after that as their own possession. They have to keep the edges soft and the head polished. If you drop it or someone uses it to hammer a nail in by mistake, you've got to polish off the face…'

The purpose of the leather hammer is to spread the force of the blow to create an even surface

The Tool With No Name
fit for (any) purpose

'I tend to prefer hand tools rather than using power. If you have to plug it in then something can go wrong with it'

Improvisation – and the old adage of necessity being the mother of invention – means that often the best tool for the job will have been intended for a different purpose entirely.

This double-bladed tool is an artist's implement – most likely for use with pigments or for applying oil paint. For Lola Lely, a multi-disciplinary designer, its role depends entirely upon what work she's currently engaged in. 'I call it whatever job I need it for,' she explains. 'So I'll say, "Can you pass the spoon?" and people in the studio will say, "What spoon?" But when I need it to stir something, I'll call it the stirrer instead! It's so adaptable and versatile.'

Having trained originally as a tattoo artist – a trade she practised in Mexico – Lely took a furniture-making course before going on to the Royal College of Art in London, where she studied the theory of design. Following a commission from The New Craftsmen for a project called The Makers Table, where she experimented with natural dyes on wood (using the tannin in the wood itself to stain the piece) she became more interested in working with dyes, paints and pigments, combining them with other natural materials.

It was at this point that her need for a multi-purpose tool was satisfied. 'I have no idea what its intended use is,' she admits. 'I spotted it in an old art shop in Florence years ago, so it must be used by artists. But when I saw it I thought it would make a really good stirrer-cum-spatula-cum-cutting-and-pressing tool. It's also good for grinding pigments.'

Due to the nature of her work, Lely tends to pick up potential tools continuously. And while there is a wide range of purpose-made tongs for dyeing available commercially, she finds she actually tends to use 'a bunch of sticks' instead. But this instrument offers more possibilities – with the job dictating its role rather than vice versa. 'I really like hardware stores and art supply shops,' she says. 'Sometimes I won't know what the intention is – what the tool is actually for – but I can see how it would be useful to me. It's been an ongoing research project, and I've found different tools that I've adapted along the way. I still use my woodworking tools, but I've probably ruined them now by using them for the wrong things. I use all sorts of utensils for my work, but there are certain ones that I like using more than others – and I tend to prefer hand tools rather than using power. If you have to plug it in then something can go wrong with it.'

Made from a single bar of stainless steel, the 'tool with no name' has been flattened at both ends; one end is slightly more tapered and the other fatter

'I have no idea what its intended use is… I thought it would make a really good stirrer-cum-spatula-cum-cutting-and-pressing tool. It's also good for grinding pigments'

in shape. 'It's got quite sharp edges, so if you sharpen it more you can use it to chop up roots for dyeing, so it's also my Stanley knife,' says Lely. 'It's flat-wrought, but something's been done to it – it's been flattened and faceted so that you can hold it and it doesn't roll out of your hand. But it's not been done evenly, so you can tell it's not been done by machine. That's a good thing, because it makes it ergonomic.'

Because she creates her dyes herself, Lely's work requires chopping raw material, grinding it, picking up measured amounts, stirring it to dissolve it and also manipulating cloth and other materials to be dyed. Each one of these stages would usually require a highly specific – if simple – tool. 'So, for example, madder comes in root form, which is a really powerful orange colour, and you cut it down and dry it out, and only once it's dry can you grind it into a powder. You make lots of it and put it into a jar – which you then measure out when you need it. And because I don't use measuring spoons, I use what I would then call "the spatula", which is also the knife I used to cut it up with… it's my Swiss Army knife in a way…'

The differing sizes of the flattened blade shapes at each end are also useful when Lely is measuring out quantities of her ground dye. 'So the thinner end is the equivalent of a teaspoon and the fat side is a tablespoon. But because it's flat it's much better to use than a spoon – whenever you tip the powder into the jar using it, whatever's on there just slides straight off and you know you've got an exact amount; nothing is left behind as can happen with the rounded cross-section of a spoon.'

Once the dye is in place in her glass mixing jar, the tool adopts yet another role, as Lely describes: 'Because one end has got a pointed tip, you can use it to really get into the corners when you're dissolving dyes in a jar – to reach the nooks and crannies and the very bottom of the jar to get all the pigment dissolved. Again, it's much better than a spoon, which is too rounded to do the job properly.'

Care and maintenance is minimal: 'I sharpen it and oil it a little bit,' says Lely. 'I never wash it, I just wipe it with a little bit of oil. Because it's stainless steel it never tarnishes – you just wipe it off – so you can actually use that one tool for all the dyes, whereas often you need one for indigo, one for madder, one for cochineal… also, having only one tool, I'm less likely to lose it because I know I have to look after it, whereas if I have loads they always go missing!'

As you might expect of a versatile designer-maker, Lely is keen to make her own version of the tool in the future, with a few personalised tweaks. Through her practical eyes, it's a relatively simple task. 'You'd just have to get the metal really hot and hammer each end,' she says. 'The only thing I would change is it could be a bit longer: you don't want to contaminate dyes with the sweat and grease from your hands; likewise indigo particularly can really stain your fingernails. Sometimes if I'm using a tall jar it's not quite long enough… because obviously its purpose was originally something else, and ideally I'd want to have a really long stirrer: 35cm long would be great; this is only 18cm.' She did consider cutting it in half and then adding an extension to it – a trick she is used to, having customised her tattoo needles in her previous career by soldering a length of metal to them – but since the tool is made from stainless steel, it's harder to simply weld a longer handle to it. Furthermore, she's respectful of the fact it is a unique handmade piece, 'and I wouldn't really want to ruin someone else's handiwork'.

The Kolinsky Sable Brush

hairs and graces

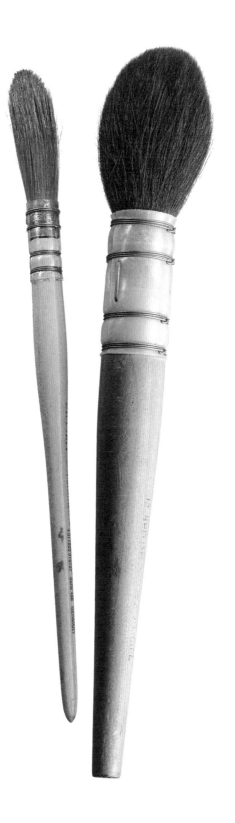

'I only use red kolinsky sable brushes… They hold the medium so
well. It's an extension of you'

The uses of the brush are many and various. In order to accurately summarise its importance as a tool, you'd have to find a dozen craftsmen, employed in various trades, to explain the subtleties of its use.

Fortunately, we found Colin Mullins. Specialising in gilding and the restoration of metalwork using specialist paint systems, Mullins has built a reputation as one of the leading conservators of historical buildings in the United Kingdom. The list of projects he has undertaken includes Buckingham Palace, Westminster Abbey and the Houses of Parliament. He's also a dab hand at coats of arms. And for all of these jobs, the brush is fundamental. 'Brushes to me are really important,' he says. 'I use them for lots of different mediums – oil, water, gouache… whatever I'm using, whether it's wall paintings right through to gilding, marbling, graining, paper hanging…'

While Mullins stands as a shining beacon for the importance of traditional craftsmen's skills, it's the quality of the tool that he puts above all else. 'With my gilding items, whether I'm doing work in gold, platinum or palladium, I only use red kolinsky sable brushes,' he says. Produced using only the hair from the tail of the male kolinsky sable (*Mustela sibirica*) – this adds a certain premium to the cost of producing them. For a start, the animal – a species of weasel – doesn't thrive well in captivity, and is found only in Siberia. Furthermore, there is usually a set season for gathering kolinsky hair, since it grows thicker on the tail in the winter months.

'They're hugely expensive and they take a long time to make,' says Mullins. But, for him, it's the only option. 'They hold the medium so well. It's an extension of you, because you're trying to produce something really clean, and that's what it gives you.'

And, at the level at which Mullins operates, acquiring brushes isn't simply a case of walking into the local hardware store: instead, he has them made bespoke, to his exact requirements. 'Years ago, artisans would always make their own tools anyway,' he reasons. 'Then in later years you ended up with brush manufacturers who would make to a high end. There's only a few real manufacturers these days who make brushes at the quality I'd actually want to use. But they're very expensive, because of the way natural hair behaves. You can get synthetic alternatives, but natural hair is the best thing for holding oils for instance – it absorbs into the hair to give you that better finish. It is a huge difference compared with a cheap brush.'

Mullins' favoured brush maker is Da Vinci, based in Nuremberg. 'They're about the best brush on the market today,' he says. 'I've had other independents make brushes for me, but you want that consistency. I still sometimes make some myself to suit whatever purposes I need. So I'll get a brush, pull it apart, take the hair out and remake a new brush for myself.'

But when he has a new brush made by someone else, Mullins will first check it to make sure that, not only is the overall quality to his standards, it is set correctly in the ferule ('the shiny bit' that connects the handle to the brush end). 'You used to find a wooden stop that they'd bind in between the brush hair,' he explains. 'So say the hair length is four inches long in total, they'd bend it in a machine so that it's folded over, bent in the middle, and it's then held with a wedge in the middle, so that gives you a reservoir to take the medium that you're using the brush with. So that helps it to hold and absorb the paint or whatever it is you're using.'

At this point, things become (more) confusing. Because, adopting the vernacular of the artisan, Mullins doesn't in fact refer to his preferred tools as brushes at all – but rather 'pencils'. 'Usually for my gilding work I won't use a pointed brush, which is known as a point or pointer, I'll use semi-dome brushes. A lot of artisans will call them pencils, because we hold them like a pencil. So for gilding purposes, I prefer a kolinsky domed brush that I have specially made.'

As well as being well made with good-quality hair, there also has to be plenty of it. 'That's the main problem,' says Mullins. 'The cheap brushes don't tend to have a lot of hair. When I get new brushes, the first thing I tend to do is wash them out – in detergent first, but then oil them up, so they've got the oil back in them. The reason for washing them is to get all the loose bits out, because new brushes will always have loose particles. Once you've done that, first you dry them out with a nice cotton rag to start and then just let them dry in the air.'

The oiling-up process is a disarmingly basic one: Mullins wipes the brush in the palm of his hand, rotating the handle to pick up natural oils and grease from the skin 'to clean it and work it out, so the brush becomes more active'. Commercial gilders, he notes, will often use a bit of goose fat, or Vaseline, to aid them in picking up gold leaf rather than relying on static alone.

'A lot of gilders used to grow a bit of stubble on their face or a bit of a short beard – the blokes, obviously – and they'd put a bit of Vaseline in that, and then they'd wipe the brush or gilder's tip against it.'

As for the old proverb that a bad workman always blames his tools, Mullins has the perfect riposte: good workmen don't buy bad tools. 'I've always found over the years – it's nearly 50 years now – you should always buy the best you can. I'd always say that if you're trying to advise artisans: buy the best kit you can afford. Or at least start out with something good quality and build up to the best. It's the same with materials, because the tools of your trade are also the materials that you use. If you buy bad-quality stuff – bad brushes and bad kit – you won't get a good result. But if you get good quality, it will (a) last longer – as long as you keep them correctly – and (b) the materials will work better with really good kit and make your job easier.'

That said, even the best brushes have a limit. 'I'm wearing them all out now,' says Mullins. 'Some of my brushes are really tatty. But if you have a brush for 40 years, it will last well as long as you look after it, but it does get dog-eared around the edges. You can scissor them to keep the shape, but then you lose the quality of the brush, and it reaches a point where you can't really use it. I'll often still have it in my kit though, because I don't want to get rid of it.'

Mullins estimates that over the years he's gone through a thousand brushes in total. He's not particularly sentimental about individual brushes but admits that, 'There's a couple that I wouldn't cast as lucky, but they're my favoured brushes: they seem to do the right job at the right time, so they're the ones you'll go to more often than not. They vary enormously. At any one time I'll have probably 50–60 different types of brushes. Maybe more. And I'll always have 20–30 on my table. It drives my wife mad, there's brushes everywhere. I suppose it might be a bit of an addiction to be honest with you. I can't pass one by if I see a really good one for sale, that is the big trouble: "I need that one for this job…!" But generally at this level, with people who are making brushes bespoke for you, you'll go into detail and talk through exactly what it is you want, and then trial it. You're talking a lot of money here. Normal people wouldn't think of spending that amount on a brush. You could get a small moped for the same amount.'

The price is worth it though. 'It's so important, it is an extension of your hand. I mean your hand is really your most valuable tool – that and your eye – but beyond hand-eye coordination, the brush is the most valuable to me.'

The Ulu
following the Arctic curve

The ulu is an all-purpose knife traditionally used by communities in the extreme north of countries bordering the Arctic Circle: in particular the Inuit (found in Canada, Greenland and Alaska) and the Yupik and Aleut peoples (native to Alaska and Russia). It is used for skinning animals and cleaning their hides as well as cutting food, trimming blocks of ice and even for cutting children's hair. Occasionally it can also be used as a weapon.

Traditionally it has a curved steel blade, similar in shape to a herb chopper, with a single handle running parallel to the blade's edge, typically made from caribou antler, walrus ivory, musk-ox horn or hardwood. This design ensures that the force applied by the user is centred over the middle of the blade, which helps when cutting bone and other hard materials, and is used with a rocking motion, just as in chopping herbs.

Examples of the ulu (also known as the *sakiaq* or *saakiq* in Tunumiit, the language of East Greenland, and *kegginalek* among the Yupik) have been found dating back to 2,500BC. Originally the blade would have been made of slate, as smelting technology was not practised in the Arctic. Examples with copper blades have also been found in the Northern Territories, but these days the blade is often made simply by cutting a hand-saw into shape.

This particular model was made by leatherworker and designer Mark Tallowin, who specialises in making bags under the brand name Tallowin. 'This is the first knife I ever made, before I'd even begun working in leather,' he says. 'In many ways it's the tool that set me on my current path. It was forged years ago while I was living in the desert of West Texas. I used an old charcoal forge, a rusty engineer's hammer and a chunk of train track for an anvil – a crude but effective combination.'

The handle is made from a simple carved block of ebony, with a copper pin used to secure it to the blade (Tallowin explains that a local Texan gunsmith helped him to set it). 'When it was complete, it needed a sheath to protect the blade, so I started work on a simple sleeve using some leather offcuts a friend gave me. I immediately realised how fascinating a material leather is – both supple and strong, flexible and tough at the same time. Before long the leatherwork took over and this obsession continues to this day,' he says. 'I keep that sleeve, in all its crudeness, as a reminder of where my path with this incredible material began.'

Although based on the traditional ulu, Tallowin's version has a much slower

Examples of the ulu have been found dating back to 2,500BC

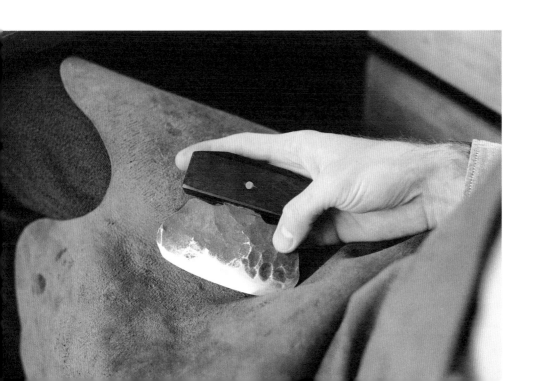

'The unusual design, with the handle set directly above the blade, means you have great power and control behind a pushing cut'

curve to its edge than the originals, since he uses it for cutting firm leather on a solid surface, as opposed to cleaning caribou and seal skins stretched on frames. 'The unusual design, with the handle set directly above the blade, means you have great power and control behind a pushing cut,' he explains. 'It's built solidly where the steel meets the handle, but it's forged nice and thin towards the edge, so it can slide through thick hide with ease.'

As well as using his improvised ulu as a guillotine with a gentle rolling action, Tallowin also uses it to cut leather by sliding the knife along its length. 'It's not a tool I use every day, but when I need to make laser-straight cuts in thick leather, nothing beats it,' he explains. 'This is when the solidity and length of the blade comes into its own – the long edge acts almost like a rudder-board in a boat, keeping it straight and true. Of course what makes it perfect for straight lines makes it useless for tight curves – imagine trying to figure-skate in a pair of skis.'

Consequently, Tallowin will often switch between a handful of different specialist knives when working on a single leather pattern, each suited to its own particular job. 'Making a tool for a single task means you can refine it physically as you clarify its purpose,' he explains. 'This knife has been ground down many times since I first forged it, for instance. You can continue to fine-tune the cross-section and hone the edge as the years go. The rate of change slows down but never stops – perfection is always strived for but never quite achieved. That shouldn't stop you trying though.'

As for care, Tallowin says he keeps the knife 'scarily sharp'. (But adds, 'the old adage about a blunt knife being more dangerous than a sharp one is true.') This means that great care has to be taken when using it to ensure no accidents occur – particularly with an instrument specifically designed to cut through bone. 'You've got to keep your wits about you when using it, of course, but that's a good guiding principle anyway,' says Tallowin. 'As someone who makes his living with his hands, you soon come to realise that it's your hands that are the most precious tools you have…'

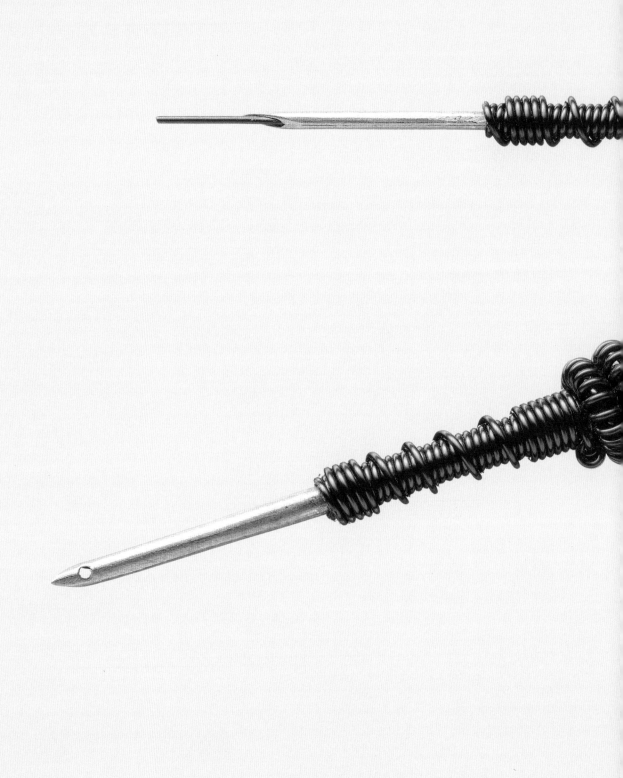

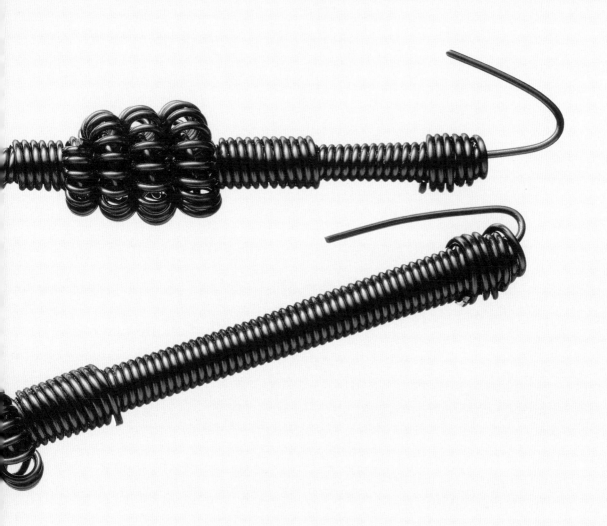

Needlepunch Needles
the needle and the pattern done

Needlepunch is the craft of looping yarn or ribbon in a pattern through fabric; a technique that typically involves punching a pattern with needles using a carding process. In the UK, it is almost entirely a machine-driven technique beyond the odd amateur enthusiast.

'I didn't know about this process at all,' says John Allen, a textile designer specialising in printed, woven and knitted fabrics for more than 25 years and who was instrumental in setting up the knitting department at the Royal College of Art in London in 1977, where he was organising tutor until 1989. 'I only discovered it after I retired in 1995. I don't know anywhere in the UK where people teach it. I do know a few people who do it themselves, because they've asked me for needles. And I know a woman up in Orkney called Ingrid Tait – she has a company called Tait & Style – who bought the only machine I know of from somewhere in Huddersfield, using a grant from the Crafts Council. I've got a piece I did on her machine.'

Tait reveals she first discovered needlepunching while doing a spinning course at Huddersfield Polytechnic, but found it was being used for 'dated and uninspired' work – not least to produce insulation materials and wadding – and saw its potential for use in fashion. She has since produced scarves for Liberty and Paul Smith, as well as through her own brand. Likewise, Allen (something of a legend in British fashion circles, having taught several generations of designers who have gone on to become household names) has produced collaborations using the technique himself – including with Jonathan Anderson for Loewe.

Given the scarcity of examples of the work in the UK, Allen outsources the production of his designs to specialist artisan makers in Nepal – which is where he found these incredible, intricately made needles. 'I learnt how to do it myself,' says Allen, 'and then I found these people on the temple steps in Kathmandu – they work in the open all year round – there's just two of them, a father and son, who just sit there selling the needles and embroidery plates and silks.'

Allen's discovery has resulted in a hugely successful second career following his retirement from academia: producing designs that are then turned into wall hangings that resemble tapestries – although he insists they should properly be described as 'carpets for walls', since the technique involved is more akin to carpet making than tapestry.

'You do the outline with the small one and then you fill in with the big one'

'The needles are decorated with wire – which provides shape and prevents you from pushing them too far into the fabric'

'I draw out the design and then they actually work it from my drawings,' he explains. 'Sometimes I'll draw direct on fabric, sometimes I'll draw on paper and they'll transfer it onto fabric. But they had previously only done traditional ethnic Nepalese designs, so they find mine quite strange. I have to give them quite clear instructions otherwise it can come back looking quite wacky!'

The unusual shape of the needle – with a small bulbous part below where it is held – is to ensure it will only penetrate so far when pushed into the fabric (typically a stiff, open weave is used as a canvas). When it reaches the fabric, you pull the needle back up, producing loops… 'and then you go up and down, up and down,' explains Allen, mimicking the repetitive process that explains why it has largely become mechanised in modern manufacture. The process leaves a loop on the reverse side. 'So when you've finished it, on the front side it looks like stitchery, but when you turn it over it looks like looped velvet. You then cut that side and it becomes smooth, like velvet. It's the most beautiful surface. The loops make the image look fuzzy, and it's only when you cut them that the perfect image emerges. You just hold your scissors flat to the surface, and cut away – it's like cutting grass with shears. It couldn't be done in the same way by machine.'

Other than scissors, only two other tools are required in the entire process – the two needles that, while they may look very similar, differ slightly in size. 'You do the outline with the small one and then you fill in with the big one,' says Allen, matter-of-factly. The needles are – of course – handmade, with copper wire wrapped around a central metal needle, which has a hollow interior. The metal is sharpened to a needlepoint at one end and a flat end at the other, and then decorated with wire – which also provides shape and that prevents you from pushing them too far into the fabric.

'They are beautiful things,' says Allen. 'The tool is a work of art in itself. Of course, because they're handmade they're all individual and unique. I wouldn't mind buying a lot of them and framing them…'

The Gilder's Tip
all that glisters

Any work involving the use of gold leaf raises its own unique set of challenges. It is so light it can easily be lifted up by the slightest air current, folding over on itself, and is prone to disintegrate under the slightest touch. 'Gold leaf is very delicate,' says Emma Peascod, a gilding and *verre églomisé* expert who specialises in producing 'surface design' work in reflective materials. 'It can be torn easily, floats like a feather and will stick to everything that you don't want it to stick to.'

Even picking up gold leaf to do any sort of work with it poses problems, which is where the gilder's tip comes in. A wide, flat brush made of squirrel hair, it is held in a cardboard sheath that serves as a handle. The long, fine bristles are designed to lift the gold (or silver) leaf from the leather cutting pad and transport it safely to the surface you are working on, using a combination of grease and static electricity. Although Vaseline can be used as the agent, Peascod will often simply brush the tip against her face or neck, coating the brush hairs with enough natural oil from her skin to do the job. She will then waft the gilder's tip over the leaf in one smooth, fluid movement, lifting it into the air and floating it down into position on the working surface.

'You have to "load" the tip with grease and static in order to pick up the leaf you are working with,' Peascod explains. 'Getting the right amount of grease and/or static takes time. Gold leaf is very light compared to silver, so needs less encouragement to stick to the bristles. If you have too much grease, then the leaf won't leave your tip onto the place where you intend it to go. I find that wiping the brush against my cheek collects up just enough grease and static – it becomes a bit of a tick that I do between placing each leaf. When people visit the studio I forget I'm doing it and I'm sure people think I'm just playing with the lovely soft squirrel hairs…'

Although *verre églomisé* was popularised in France in the 18th century (thanks largely to the work of Jean Baptiste Glomy, picture-framer to Louis XV), it is a skill that has been known since pre-Roman times. The purist style of *verre églomisé* involves gilding the back of a piece of glass all over and – once it's dry – scratching into the gilded surface and 'back-painting' it.

'You see it in French shop fronts, bar fronts and pharmacies,' says Peascod. 'You literally scratch or engrave a design into the gold.' (The art of gilding itself can be traced back to Ancient Egypt: writing in the 5th century BC,

The long fine bristles are designed to lift the gold or silver leaf from the cutting pad and transport it to the surface you are working on, via a combination of grease and static

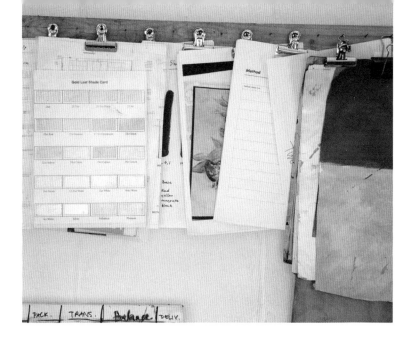

'Gold leaf is very delicate. It can be
torn easily, floats like a feather and
will stick to everything that you don't
want it to stick to'

the Greek historian Herodotus records the Egyptian practice of gilding metal and wood. In Europe, incidentally, silver-gilt has always been more common.)

By 'playing around' with different textures and layers of painting, Peascod produces different surfaces; each design changing subtly – and sometimes dramatically – according to how the light catches them. The 'eureka' moment that resulted in her forming her design company, Studio Peascod, was in applying traditional Japanese papers as a backing to her *verre églomisé* work. (This was a skill she picked up on a working trip to rural Japan to learn a traditional paper-making technique, involving washing the fibres in ice-cold water in order to separate two types of bark, removing any impurities to produce a white fibre.)

Despite being a very basic tool, the gilder's tip is essential for the water-gilding work with gold leaf that Peascod specialises in. 'It would be extremely challenging to water gild onto glass without this brush,' she explains. 'In Japan, gold leaf is picked up with bamboo tweezers, but mainly to place onto a paper or wood surface and with a tackier side – or with glue. I don't think I could do *verre églomisé* with tweezers.'

Although the design of the gilder's tip has remained much the same over the centuries, with different lengths and thicknesses of brush available according to preference, there have been some significant developments and improvements over time; Peascod cites the Smith Tip by 'glass gilder extraordinaire' David Smith, which has extra-long hairs designed to pick up full sheets of gold more easily. Badger hair and pony hair are also commonly used, while synthetic hair tips are also available for those who don't wish to use animal hair. The transparent Thorn Tip, meanwhile, allows you to see through the tool in order to lay leaf more accurately.

Peascod emphasises, however, that no design is intrinsically better than another. 'I think it's personal. The one pictured here is not a special version, it's just that this particular one has, for me, the right amount of bristles and length to it.'

She has, however, adapted and personalised her tools to suit her working style. 'A long time ago I attached a small cardboard addition with masking tape in order to hold the tip,' she says. 'A friend and experienced gilder showed me that trick – I still use it when doing large flat surfaces. I have cut down the length of the bristles on some tips – since shorter hairs work well on small pieces – and I've also cut down a tip widthways to create a narrower end to the bristles, which is good to get into narrow spaces or for picking up narrower pieces. That's the beauty of them being held together with cardboard: they are easy to adjust as you wish.'

BILLY LLOYD (*The Turning Tool, page 136*) is an award-wining designer and maker of ceramics for daily use.
billylloyd.co.uk

CHRISTOPHER HOWE (*Collections 06: Upholstery, page 162*) is a furniture maker, antiques dealer, restorer, fabric expert and interior designer.
howelondon.com

CHRISTOPHER KING (*The Drawknife, page 42*) is a master batmaker, designer and photographer at Gray-Nicolls.
gray-nicolls.co.uk

COLIN MULLINS (*The Kolinsky Sable Brush*, *page 178*) is a historical gilder and colour expert, specialising in gilding and the restoration of metalwork using specialist paint systems.
ukgilder.com

DAVID LINLEY, 2nd Earl of Snowdon (*The Plane*, *page 52*), is the founder of the brand Linley, specialising in marquetry, cabinetmaking, bespoke furniture, upholstery and interior design.
davidlinley.com

EMMA DAVIES (*The Widger*, *page 28*) is the co-owner of the Walled Nursery with her husband Monty Davies.
thewallednursery.com

EMMA PEASCOD (*The Gilder's Tip*, *page 196*) is an expert in gilding and the production of reflective surfaces.
studiopeascod.com

FERGUS GARRETT (*The Tickling Fork*, *page 108*) is the chief executive of the Great Dixter Charitable Trust, where he was formerly head gardener.
greatdixter.co.uk

FLORIAN GADSBY (*Collections 03: Ceramics*, *page 100*) is renowned potter.
floriangadsby.com

GARETH NEAL (*The Cordless Power Drill*, *page 66*) is a contemporary furniture maker whose design studio incorporates digital and traditional fabrication techniques.
garethneal.co.uk

GAZE BURVILL (*Collections 01: Carpentry*, *page 50*) are specialists in outdoor furniture, working primarily in oak and chestnut.
gazeburvill.com

GEOFFRY POWELL (1920-99) (*Collections 02: Architecture*, *page 72*) was the founding partner of Chamberlin, Powell and Bon, leading British post-war architects of The Barbican, Golden Lane, Leeds University and other important listed buildings.

JAKE SUTTON (*The Vernier Caliper, page 122*) is an artist, inventor, set designer and horologist/clockmaker.
jakesutton.co.uk

JIM PARKYN (*The Whalebone Sculpting Tool, page 88*) is senior model maker at Aardman Animations.
aardman.com

JOHN ALLEN (*Needlepunch Needles, page 190*) has been a textile designer specialising in printed, woven and knitted fabrics for more than 25 years. In 1977, he was instrumental in setting up the knitting department at the Royal College of Art in London where he was organising tutor until 1989.
john-allen-london.co.uk

LINDA BROTHWELL (*Tools: An Appreciation, page 12*) is an artist and maker who collects and researches tools and their uses.
lindabrothwell.com

LOLA LELY (*The Tool With No Name, page 170*) is a multi-disciplinary designer-maker who collaborates with a wide variety of experts in fields as diverse as cookery, anthropology and storytelling.
lolalely.com

LONDON GLASSBLOWING (*Collections 05: Glass Making, page 134*) is the first hot-glass studio in Europe, founded by Peter Layton in 1976.
londonglassworks.com

MARK TALLOWIN (*The Ulu, page 184*) is a leather designer specialising in handbags and wallets, all made entirely by his own hand alone.
marktallowin.co.uk

NDIDI EKUBIA (*The Silver Hammer, page 96*) is a silversmith who utilises traditional hand-raising techniques in her work.
ndidiekubia.com

PEDRO DA COSTA FELGUEIRAS (*The Pestle and Mortar, page 148*) is a world-respected expert in traditional paint and lacquer techniques, who established Lacquer Studios in 1995.
lacquerstudios.com

PETER LAYTON (*Glassmaking Jacks, page 102*) is one of the world's leading artists working in glass and the founder, in 1976, of the London Glassblowing gallery and studio – the first hot-glass studios in Europe.
londonglassworks.com

RHS GARDENS (*Collections 04: Gardening, page 116*)
Founded by the Royal Horticultural Society, the world's leading garden charity, RHS Gardens showcase the best gardening in the UK via four principal gardens: Wisley in Surrey, Rosemoor in Devon, Hyde Hall in Essex and Harlow Carr in North Yorkshire.
rhs.org.uk

ROBIN WOOD (*The Turning Hook, page 74*) is a master woodturner and the founding chairman of the Heritage Crafts Association.
robin-wood.co.uk

RON GEESIN (*The Collector, page 18*) is a composer who collects adjustable spanners dating from 1970 or earlier.
rongeesin.com

SEAN SUTCLIFFE (*The Chisel, page 34*) is the co-founder (with Sir Terence Conran) of contemporary furniture makers Benchmark.
benchmarkfurniture.com

TROY SCOTT SMITH (*The Onion Hoe, page 118*) is the head gardener at Sissinghurst Castle Garden.
nationaltrust.org.uk/sissinghurst-castle-garden

ZOE BRADLEY (*The Bradawl, page 144*) is an artist specialising in paper as a medium across many disciplines, having trained in fashion and apprenticed for Alexander McQueen.
zoebradley.com

Lol Keegan, *lolkeegan.com*
Pages 10, 29, 32, 34–35, 41, 43, 48, 51, 52–53, 56, 59, 66–67, 73, 75, 76, 81, 88–89, 95, 97, 101, 102–103, 109, 115, 117, 118–119, 123, 127, 128–129, 135, 136–137, 144–145, 149, 156–157, 163, 164–165, 171, 178–179, 180, 185, 190–191, 196–197, 198

Chloë Winstanley, *chloe-winstanley.com*
Pages 3, 4–5, 13, 16, 17, 60, 62, 65, 69, 70, 84, 85, 106, 107, 139, 140, 151, 152, 153, 154, 166, 168, 169, 172, 174, 175, 177, 187, 188, 193, 194

Julian Anderson, *juliananderson.co.uk*
Pages 44, 47, 111, 112

Louise Long, *louiselong.co.uk*
Pages 131, 132, 159, 160

Sam Walton
Pages 91, 92, 200, 201, 203

Katya de Grunwald, *katyadegrunwald.com*
Pages 19, 21, 22

Image courtesy of Benchmark Furniture
Page 38

Petr Krejci, *www.petrkrejci.com*
Page 37, 38

Aaron Hargreaves, *fosterandpartners.com*
Page 40

All words and interviews by Mark Hooper unless otherwise credited.